Women and Men in Scripture and the Church

Women and Men in Scripture and the Church

A Guide to the Key Issues

Edited by

Steven Croft and Paula Gooder

CANTERBURY
PRESS
Norwich

© the contributors 2013

First published in 2013 by the Canterbury Press Norwich

Editorial office
3rd Floor, Invicta House,
108–114 Golden Lane,
London EC1Y 0TG

Canterbury Press is an imprint of Hymns Ancient & Modern Ltd
(a registered charity)
13A Hellesdon Park Road, Norwich,
Norfolk, NR6 5DR, UK

www.canterburypress.co.uk

Scripture quotations are from the New Revised Standard Version of the
Bible, Anglicized Edition, copyright 1989, 1995 by the Division of Christian
Education of the National Council of the Churches of Christ in the USA.
Used by permission. All rights reserved.

British Library Cataloguing in Publication data

A catalogue record for this book is available
from the British Library

978 1 84825 510 4

Typeset by Regent Typesetting
Printed and bound in Great Britain by
CPI Group (UK) Ltd, Croydon

Contents

The Lord is Risen!

On the first Easter Day, according to all four Gospels, the first witnesses of the resurrection were women. Their names are recorded. All the Gospels agree that Mary Magdalene was there, and some also add the presence of Joanna, Mary the mother of James, and Salome (Matthew 28.1; Mark 16.1; Luke 24.10; John 20.1). Luke also talks about other women as well (Luke 24.10).

The women are witnesses in two important senses. They are the first eyewitnesses of the resurrection. They see that the stone is rolled away, the tomb is empty, the graveclothes are folded and placed on one side. They see and speak with the risen Lord.

But this group of women are witnesses in a second sense as well. They are specifically commanded by angels and by Jesus himself to go and tell others the good news. They are sent by the Lord as apostles and commanded to speak as evangelists.

According to Matthew, the angels give this commission: 'Go quickly and tell his disciples, "He has been raised from the dead"' (28.7), and this is underlined by Jesus: 'Go and tell my brothers to go to Galilee' (28.10). According to Mark, the women are told: 'Go and tell his disciples and Peter' (16.7). Luke tells us twice that the women told the disciples what had happened (24.9 and 23). John focuses on Jesus' words to Mary Magdalene:

'But go to my brothers and say to them, I am ascending to my Father and your Father, to my God and your God.' Mary Magdalene went and announced to the disciples: 'I have seen the Lord.'

Ponder this truth for a moment. What does it say about the place of women in the Christian faith that they were beyond doubt the first witnesses of the resurrection and the first to carry the good news? Remember that in the culture of the day, women were not considered equal to men in terms of politics or law or social status. They were regarded as less reliable witnesses. These passages from the Gospels are remarkable as a testimony to the importance of the role of women in the life and ministry of God's people and in the Church of Jesus Christ.

Women and men in ministry today

Women went on to exercise a significant ministry in the life of the early Church, as we shall see. But as seen in the New Testament, a debate began in the very earliest days of the Church about the respective roles of women and men in society, church and family. That debate continues to this day.

Within the Church of England it has focused on whether and how women should be able to take up different roles within the lay and ordained ministry of the Church. Women were first admitted as Readers in 1969 (apart from a brief period during the First World War), ordained as deacons in 1987 and as priests in 1994.

For the past 12 years, the Church of England has been debating legislation to enable women to be ordained as bishops. A measure to enable this to happen was debated by the General Synod on 20 November 2012. The vast majority of bishops voted in favour of the measure, as did 75 per cent of the clergy. Of the House of Laity, 62 per cent were also in favour. However, this fell short of the two-thirds majority required and so the measure was defeated, although it is hoped that new legislation to enable women to become bishops will return to the Synod very soon.

The Synod debate revealed a need for resources to help churches and congregations to look again at the question of women and men in the Scriptures. Many of those who opposed the measure did so from a conviction that it is more 'biblical' to argue that women should not become bishops or exercise authority over men in the life of the Church or the family. In fact their view is simply one way of interpreting the Scriptures and gives priority to just a small number of contested passages.

The aim of this book is to help individual Christians, small groups and even whole churches to look again honestly and carefully at what the Bible says about women and men in family life, in ministry and in society. It is written by people who all believe that it *is* 'biblical' for women to serve the Church in many different ways, including through preaching and teaching and through being ordained as bishops, priests and deacons. We hope that using this book will help many people respond to the very deep feelings stirred up by the outcome of the General Synod debate, through study, prayer and conversation. As the debate moves forward in the Church of England, it must be about more than a process to keep everyone together. We must also examine what we believe.

And we believe that many Christians, men and women, are looking for fresh ways to answer the questions of the society around us as to what the Christian faith teaches about gender and equality.

Interpreting the Bible

One of the real challenges for this subject is the question of how we interpret the Bible. Again, sometimes the debate about women in ministry can caricature those who believe that women's full involvement in ministry is biblical as twisting the text to suit their own purposes; whereas those who hold the opposing view take it at face value. The reality is that our reading of the Bible is always much more complex than that. When we come to the text all of us, no matter who we are, bring 'baggage'. It is amazing how hard it is even to see what the text really says, especially if you know it well already, let alone to work out what it might mean. The problem is that biblical interpretation is not an exact science – two people can come to the text with full integrity, using the best tools available, and can still end up with widely differing interpretations.

A helpful rule of thumb is to ask three key questions whenever we read the Bible:

- What can we know about the historical situation of the time and what might this tell us about what the authors meant and why they said it?

- What does the text actually say (sometimes this requires looking at more than one translation so that you can hear the words afresh in a slightly different form)?

- What am I bringing to this text? What hopes, expectations, fears and so on are going to affect the way I am reading this particular text?

However, we need to remember that it is possible to read the Bible in different ways. As the authors of this book, we all believe that our position on women's ministry legitimately arises from a faithful reading of the Bible, not by twisting the text to suit our own purposes but by asking these three questions as we seek to understand more fully some of the key passages involved in this debate.

Good news

We believe that the account given in the Bible of the role of women and men in God's purposes is profoundly good news for humankind. It is an account that affirms the equality and status of both men and women and their call to partnership in society and family life and in the Church. It is an account that is radically different from many others in ancient society and down the ages. It is good news that liberates women from subservience to men and also sets men free from gender stereotypes.

The Christian church is an imperfect institution. It has not always lived out or practised the message of the Scriptures. However, the Bible's account of gender is liberating good news for older women who may have grown up with the idea that they are called by God to be subservient or to restrict their life choices. It is good news for younger Christian women considering God's call on their lives. It is good news for men, old or young, who can now work fully alongside both women and men in the service of the gospel. It is good news for the many cultures in the world where women are still treated as less than equal. It is good news for all those working in international aid or development, where the subjugation of women in culture is a major issue in combating poverty.

This debate is therefore about far more than whether or not women should exercise a particular ministry in a particular part of God's Church. It is about the ways in which we view one another as brothers and sisters within the body of Christ, about the structuring of our family life and about the ways we view society outside the Church. This is why there is such widespread interest in the Church of England's debate on the question of women bishops. We urgently need, as a Church, to recover a sense that the message of the Christian faith is good news to the society around us and good news to women and men in their relationships together.

Two arguments united in opposition

In the Church of England's debates there have been two strands of argument opposed to the ordination of women as priests and bishops. One strand argues from a particular interpretation of Scripture, and this is the focus of this short book.

The other strand argues against the ordination of women as priests and bishops on the grounds of church tradition. These developments are seen as out of step with the way the Church has ordered its ministry for hundreds of years. They are also seen as out of step with the ordering of ministry in the Roman Catholic and Orthodox Churches, where women cannot be ordained as deacons, priests or bishops. On this view, the Church of England cannot take such a weighty decision independently of these other Churches.

It is important to say at the outset that this book does not directly address these arguments from tradition (although we believe there are strong reasons for resisting them). The Church of England has taken many equally significant decisions about its life and ministry independently since the Reformation. However, we are focusing here on the Scriptures and what we believe the Bible teaches about gender.

The shape of this book

There are six chapters in this book designed for individual reading and for group study. They could also be used as the basis for a short series of sermons for a church that wanted to work through this material in its Sunday worship.

Each chapter contains an introduction that sets out the key issues, an invitation to reflect prayerfully on the biblical passage in question, a few more technical insights based on scholarship on the passage and then some longer reflections on what this might mean within the context of this debate. Each chapter ends with some questions for discussion, concluding thoughts and time for prayer.

Chapter 1 looks at the creation accounts in Genesis 1, 2 and 3 and their revolutionary message about the equal and complementary status of women.

Chapter 2 examines the way in which the New Testament builds on this in its own understanding of gender, with a particular study of Galatians 3.26–29.

Chapter 3 explores the ways in which we know women exercised ministry in the New Testament period, focusing on a study of Romans 16.

Chapter 4 looks at the three passages in the New Testament letters that appear to restrict or prohibit women from exercising authority over men or teaching: 1 Timothy 2, 1 Corinthians 11 and 14.

Chapter 5 engages with the question of the roles of women and men in family life in a number of different passages, especially Ephesians 5.

Chapter 6 explores a healthy model of service and ministry for women and men together, through study of Romans 12.

There are two brief supplementary chapters. The first gives a short history of the Church of England's exploration of the recognition of the ministry of women. The second explores some Frequently Asked Questions around this whole area.

The six main chapters are set out in a way that we hope will be helpful for small groups as well as for individuals. Some resources for prayer and reflection are included for these small groups.

In each of chapters 1–3 and 5–6, additional notes on the details of the passages have been provided by Paula Gooder.

The purpose of the book

The authors all share a conviction that the Church of England should move rapidly towards the consecration of women as bishops, and a conviction that this move is consistent with and supported by the Scriptures. We have drawn on a wide range of biblical scholarship and debate in what we have written here.

We are writing mainly for members of the Church of England, but we hope the material might be useful to those of other Churches or people in other parts of the Anglican Communion.

A proportion of the royalties from sales of this book will be given to Christian Aid to support, in particular, work among women in the developing world.

We are grateful to the different authors for writing these chapters at short notice in order to make the material available to the Church at this critical moment, and to Canterbury Press for agreeing to produce the book so quickly.

Steven Croft
Paula Gooder
January 2013

The Authors

The Rt Revd Stephen Cottrell is Bishop of Chelmsford.

The Rt Revd Dr Steven Croft is Bishop of Sheffield.

The Very Revd Viv Faull is Dean of York.

Dr Paula Gooder is a lecturer and writer in biblical studies, a Reader and member of the General Synod.

The Revd Dr Canon Joanne Grenfell is Diocesan Director of Ordinands in the Diocese of Sheffield and Residentiary Canon of Sheffield Cathedral. She has recently been appointed Archdeacon of Portsdown.

The Revd Dr Emma Ineson is tutor at Trinity College, Bristol, and a member of the General Synod.

The Revd Dr Rosalyn Murphy is vicar of St Thomas', Blackpool, a writer in biblical studies and member of the Archbishops' Council.

The Revd Dr Ian Paul is Dean of Studies at St John's College, Nottingham.

The Revd Dr Jo Bailey Wells is chaplain to the Archbishop of Canterbury at Lambeth Palace. Until recently she was the Director of the Anglican Episcopal House of Studies at Duke Divinity School.

Introductory Notes for Group Leaders

You will need a copy of this book for each member of the group. Ideally they should have the chance to read it a week or so before you begin to study it together.

Feel free to mix and match the different elements in the session to suit your own group. The material should work well with an existing home group or one that comes together after Easter or at some other time of the year.

You may need to be selective. Try to focus the time on the interactive parts of the session.

Each session should begin with the Opening Prayers on pages xxi–xxiii, which include the reading of the Scriptures.

The Bible translation used throughout is the New Revised Standard Version, Anglicized Edition.

Each chapter follows a similar structure except for Chapter 4, where there are two parts to the study. Some groups may need more time on this chapter, perhaps spreading the study over two sessions.

Different ways to use the material

An existing home group

The material is well suited to existing home groups or Bible study groups in the local church. Feel free to adapt it to your normal pattern.

Home groups linked to Sunday worship

It's possible to use the book as study material for all home groups or cell groups in the church and to link the themes to their Sunday worship. If you have ongoing home groups in your church it can be immensely helpful to connect them all together at certain times of the year and to explore the same material.

In twos and threes

Not everyone is able to be part of a small group. You could work through the material with two or three friends; or as a married couple; or as an older Christian working with someone who is new to the faith. You will need to read the chapters carefully and think about them.

On your own

Finally, the book is also intended to be read by individuals. If you are working through it on your own, make sure you use the times and spaces for prayer and for journaling.

God will be at work!

However you engage with the material, remember that God in his grace will be at work in you and in the other people who explore these passages. Be aware that for some of the group this material may be familiar and well worked through in their own lives. However, for others it may be new and, initially, disturbing as well as liberating. Be concerned to support the group as you make the journey together.

The Opening Prayers

O God, make speed to save us.
O Lord, make haste to help us.

O Lord, our governor,
How glorious is your name in all the world.

Psalm 8.1

Risen Christ,
You filled your disciples with boldness and fresh hope.
Strengthen us to proclaim your risen life.
And fill us with your peace.
To the glory of God the Father.

From *Common Worship*

O Lord, my heart is not proud;
my eyes are not raised in haughty looks.

I do not occupy myself with great matters,
with things that are too high for me.

But I have quieted and stilled my soul,
    like a weaned child on its mothers breast;
so my soul is quieted within me.

O Israel, trust in the Lord,
from this time forth and for evermore.

Psalm 131

Glory to the Father and to the Son
and to the Holy Spirit;
as it was in the beginning is now
and shall be for ever. Amen.

A short Bible reading from the passage set for the study.

For you yourself created my inmost parts;
you knit me together in my mother's womb.

I thank you, for I am fearfully and wonderfully made;
marvellous are your works, my soul knows well.

Psalm 139.12–13

Almighty God,
You have created the heavens and the earth
and made us in your own image:
teach us to discern your hand in all your works
and your likeness in all your children;
through Jesus Christ your Son our Lord;
who with you and the Holy Spirit reigns supreme over all things;
now and for ever.
Amen.

Collect for the Second Sunday before Lent

Let us bless the Lord.
Thanks be to God.

The session continues with the introduction to the study.

OPENING PRAYERS xxiii

Notes on the opening prayers

The opening prayers are based on *Common Worship*, Prayer During the Day. There is merit in using the same prayers each week while the group is looking at this material, but a different psalm and collect could be substituted. It may help to light a candle or have some other focus for prayer within the room.

1

Women and Men in the Creation and Fall Stories

Introduction

In the opening three chapters of the Bible we find the classic accounts of God's creation of the world, of God's purpose for humanity and of humanity's wilful disobedience of God. The focus begins with God – the all-powerful Creator, the origin of all things, who delights in the work of creating (and believes in taking rest too!). Most of all, God delights in the creation of humankind, with whom there is a special relationship.

Chapter 2 of the Bible focuses on that relationship, describing the many gifts and expectations God invests in humanity. Alas, chapter 3 follows with the tale of how these are tragically marred by the fall. The special relationship is not destroyed, but it is damaged – as is the relationship of man and woman to each other.

Here we explore these relationships before and during the fall: the 'vertical' relationship of humanity before God, and the 'horizontal' relationship of 'man' and 'woman' in the figures of Adam and Eve. These named individuals fulfil a representative function, both before and after the fall. Think of them as 'Every man' and 'Every woman', irrespective of individual identity, historical circumstance or geographical location. In that sense, they helpfully frame the debate concerning the place of men and women in contemporary society.

Bible study: Genesis 1.26–31

26 Then God said, 'Let us make humankind in our image, according to our likeness; and let them have dominion over the fish of the sea, and over the birds of the air, and over the cattle, and over all the wild animals of the earth, and over every creeping thing that creeps upon the earth.' 27So God created humankind in his image, in the image of God he created them; male and female he created them. 28God blessed them, and God said to them, 'Be fruitful and multiply, and fill the earth and subdue it; and have dominion over the fish of the sea and over the birds of the air and over every living thing that moves upon the earth.' 29God said, 'See, I have given you every plant yielding seed that is upon the face of all the earth, and every tree with seed in its fruit; you shall have them for food. 30And to every beast of the earth, and to every bird of the air, and to everything that creeps on the earth, everything that has the breath of life, I have given every green plant for food.' And it was so. 31God saw everything that he had made, and indeed, it was very good. And there was evening and there was morning, the sixth day.

Bible study: Genesis 2.15–25

15 The LORD God took the man and put him in the garden of Eden to till it and keep it. ¹⁶And the LORD God commanded the man, 'You may freely eat of every tree of the garden; ¹⁷but of the tree of the knowledge of good and evil you shall not eat, for in the day that you eat of it you shall die.'

18 Then the LORD God said, 'It is not good that the man should be alone; I will make him a helper as his partner.' ¹⁹So out of the ground the LORD God formed every animal of the field and every bird of the air, and brought them to the man to see what he would call them; and whatever the man called each living creature, that was its name. ²⁰The man gave names to all cattle, and to the birds of the air, and to every animal of the field; but for the man there was not found a helper as his partner. ²¹So the LORD God caused a deep sleep to fall upon the man, and he slept; then he took one of his ribs and closed up its place with flesh. ²²And the rib that the LORD God had taken from the man he made into a woman and brought her to the man. ²³Then the man said, 'This at last is bone of my bones and flesh of my flesh; this one shall be called Woman, for out of Man this one was taken.' ²⁴Therefore a man leaves his father and his mother and clings to his wife, and they become one flesh. ²⁵And the man and his wife were both naked, and were not ashamed.

Reflection together

- Read the passage a second time with different voices, perhaps reading a verse each.

- Invite everyone to say aloud a word or phrase that strikes them.

- Read the passage a third time.

- Share together what this word or phrase might mean and what questions it raises.

After reading and reflecting on both passages above:

- What differences and developments concerning the creation of humanity do you notice between Genesis chapter 1 and chapter 2?

Notes on some details of the passage

These chapters are the prologue to the story of the beginnings of the people of God. In Genesis 12, Abraham, the father of faith, is called by God. It is his response to God that begins the long journey towards the formation of God's own people. Genesis 1—11 sets up the 'pre-story' to Abraham's call, a story in which time and time again people failed to live well in the world God had made.

- We are used to calling the man and woman in Genesis 2 'Adam and Eve', but doing so muddies the picture somewhat. The Hebrew word 'Adam' is used both in Genesis 1 and Genesis 2. So in Genesis 1.26–27, where God declares his intention to make 'humankind' in his image, the Hebrew word there is 'Adam'. As a result, Genesis

1.27 says that God created Adam in his image, 'male and female he created them'. This suggests that Adam is not a specifically gendered term but a description of all human beings.

- This is supported by Genesis 2. There Adam is created but is only called a man (the Hebrew word *'is) after* the creation of the woman (*'issa*) from the rib of Adam. Thus Adam only becomes a 'man' in response to the 'woman' brought to him by God. After Eve's creation the man continues to be called Adam, but a new name is needed for his companion.

The name 'Adam' is closely related to the Hebrew word for ground or soil, 'Adamah'; the name 'Eve' is also interesting. This is the name given to the woman by Adam in Genesis 3.20. The Hebrew means life. As a result, each name tells us something important about each: Adam was formed from the dust of the ground; Eve was the source of life.

Men and women in the creation narratives

Genesis 1

God's magnificent work follows a carefully ordered progression from day to day. Each day offers increasing differentiation and sophistication, from the inanimate to the animate. The excerpt above describes the sixth day of creation – the final day of God's work – in which 'human-kind ... male and female' is brought into being.

Think of each day of this creation account like one verse of a seven-verse hymn. Each day – each verse – builds from the one before and repeats its pattern, beginning with God's word and ending with God's delight. The effect is to demonstrate the elegant simplicity and the overwhelming power with which the God-of-the-whole-universe produces beauty out of chaos and meaning out of nothingness. The testimony of praise reaches its crescendo in verse 6. We conclude that the creation of humankind is the summit of God's remarkable work and the cause of much delight. The last verse completes the picture with God resting, enjoying the fruits of six days of labour.

Note, first and foremost, how humankind is referenced and celebrated for the way in which 'it' (in the singular) bears the image of God. In this aspect, humankind is marked out as unique, underlining how special is the divine–human relationship. God is invested in the human condition and the human is entrusted with divine responsibility and authority. This is revolutionary! God is not remote, nor is humanity insignificant. From the outset, humankind is declared an agent of God; that is, it is given a key role in the purpose of God's creation.

Now this role – to exercise a ministry of responsibility over God's creation – is given to all humanity. All human persons are made in the image of God. The single entity of humanity is only subsequently described in the plural, as a community of male and female. There is no suggestion that male is created before female. Rather the opposite: 'humankind' is made in one single stroke – which, almost incidentally (as if to suggest 'of course!'), includes both genders. The responsibility to lead and rule is given to both – as part of the one community called humankind – and may not legitimately be separated according to maleness or femaleness. What matters is 'createdness' that acknowledges the Creator and 'humanness' that bears the image of God.

Yet the aspect of gender is not separable from the creation of humankind. Sexual differentiation is part of the created order and purpose from the beginning. That is to say, on the one hand, it is not part of the nature of God (unlike in the mythology of some of Israel's ancient neighbours). On the other hand, the two sexes exist from the moment humankind exists. The sexual distinction is fundamental to what it means to be human. Verse 27 ('he created them') is followed immediately by God blessing and commanding them to be fruitful and multiply, to fill the earth and subdue it – commands given to both parties, with no hint of hierarchy in their relative importance or differentiation in terms of role. Procreation can only be fulfilled by both parties functioning together! Equally, man and woman function together in ruling over the rest of creation, thus excluding the possibility of one gender claiming power over the other.

In conclusion, from the outset of Scripture we find Genesis 1 proclaiming the foundational equality and complementarity of the sexes.

Genesis 2

Beginning at Genesis 2.5 a rather different account of creation is given. This one does not present a cosmic liturgy focused on the grandeur of God, but an intense street-level reflection on the human condition. Whereas previously God created with a remote control – by his word – now God's sleeves are rolled up and the gloves removed. The potter's hands mould an 'Adam' out of soil and an 'Eve' from a rib.

At first glance it may seem that Genesis 2 is incompatible with Genesis 1. God appears to create 'man' before sending rain or establishing plants. God's charge to this man relates to the soil and the plants – not to the fish, birds and animals as before. Finally, God is concerned with man's isolation and looks for a helper – creating 'woman' subsequent to 'man', following a scan for partners among the rest of animate creation. For many the priority of man's creation denotes a hierarchical pattern in which man is in some way superior to, or in leadership over, the helper he names 'woman'.

God declares, 'It is not good that the man should be alone; I will make him a helper as his partner' (2.18). In Hebrew the term translated 'helper' does not suggest an assistant or subordinate, as in the English, but an ally, a benefactor, a companion. Most often in the Old Testament it is God who is described as the 'helper' of Israel (for example, in Exodus 18.4). This helper will be his 'partner' in the sense of being a counterpart or an opposite. She corresponds to him as his equal, both in being and function. In no way can this phrase be understood to imply male leadership or female submission as part of the created order.

Some have suggested that since the first woman was formed out of the man's rib, she is derivative, existing in a dependent and subordinate status. But Adam was also derived – from the ground – without any suggestion that the ground is superior to him. Every subsequent human is derived from woman, in the sense of birth. The notion expresses integration and solidarity, not superiority and subordination. The word 'rib' itself carries symbolic connotations of mutuality, given that it can mean 'side' as well as 'rib'.

When the man exclaims 'she shall be called woman, for out of man this one was taken' (2.27), there is a wordplay between 'woman' and 'man' ('issa and 'is in the Hebrew). These two words represent the masculine and feminine form of the same root, underlining the recognition of identity and similarity – as sexual counterparts – between these two beings. Prior to this the man has been referred to as Adam, which carries the more generic, old-fashioned sense of man as 'mortal'.

Like Genesis 1, chapter 2 contains no statement that denotes dominance and subordination, or leadership and submission, between the man and the woman. Before the fall, they are presented as fully equal in rank, with no hint of hierarchy between the genders. At creation just two authority mandates are given: God's sovereignty over humans; human authority over all the earth.

When the first of these is violated – in Genesis 3 – then the community and harmony of creation is also ruptured. The first consequence of disobedience – a discomfort with nakedness – illustrates with graphic immediacy the breakdown of trust and mutuality between the man and the woman. When God asks Adam what happened, Adam jumps to blame Eve just as Eve blames the serpent. Each passes the buck and resists responsibility. The loving harmony with each other, and between them and the rest of creation, is lost.

The consequences and punishments perhaps feel only too familiar. There is enmity – that is, hostility – between humans and animals (3.15), pain in childbirth (3.16), female desire for men and male head-ship over women (3.16), and the toil of hard labour for food (3.17). The outcome of the fall represents a disruption of God's original design for egalitarian relationship between the sexes. As a result of sin, the mutual egalitarian harmony has given way to accusation and blame. Measures are instituted that are appropriate to maintaining whatever harmony and union is still possible in the new situation. In the circum-stances of marriage, female submission and male headship might thus be understood as a temporary exercise in damage limitation, and a means by which, through God's promised blessing, full harmony – in the sense of equality without hierarchy – might again be restored along with the rest of God's original creation ideals.

For discussion

- Genesis 1 and 2 sketch the aspirational 'gold-standards' for models of human relating. What might it look like to reflect and imitate these in contemporary society? Seek examples to illustrate how these models are lived among people with whom you are acquainted.

- Genesis 3 sets out some of the problems of human relating in our sinful world. Share examples of some of the tragic realities you note in society, as well as in the Church, that correspond with the consequences of the fall, and discuss ways you might resist these patterns.

• Reflecting on Jesus' relationships in the Gospels, name some of the ways he models the God-intended norms of Genesis 1 and 2 and challenges the fall consequences of Genesis 3.

Application

On the basis of Genesis 1—3 we may attribute the tension found between the sexes – evident in the discomforts and abuses of sexual attraction, in the power dynamics of male headship, in the confinement of women and men to roles of child-rearing and food-gathering respectively – to the fall. These represent both the symptoms and consequences of human sin. It is not surprising, therefore, that we find Jesus challenging each of these less than ideal elements of human relating as he inaugurates the kingdom of God. The kingdom of God is about restoring Eden to earth: hence the importance of Genesis 1 and 2 for understanding the norms to which God's people aspire (and Genesis 3 for the ways in which God's people have gone awry).

The body of Christ is God's new creation. It is called, then, to reflect and imitate God's creation norms – across the breadth of human society and most especially in the immediate circles of family and church life. At the same time, Christians need to recognize the symptoms of the fall in all human relating. Sometimes the limitations may themselves function as a means of grace. Restoring heaven to earth is, ultimately, the work of Christ.

Closing prayers

Give thanks for God's work in creating humankind 'male and female' on the sixth day, and pray for the role and responsibilities that accompany this grace – together, to care for creation, to be fruitful, to exercise leadership and stewardship.

Spend time in remorse and confession for your participation in the fall – along with that of all men and women. Feel the shame as you receive God's anger and punishment – and allow this shame to rekindle a longing to claim more fully the harmony that is previously described and subsequently promised. Pray for a Church that dares to challenge the 'fall' models of relating according to the reversal that is brought about by Christ.

2

Humanity Redeemed in Christ

Introduction

One of the great themes of the New Testament is the new humanity we have in Christ. Because of Christ's death and resurrection, says St Paul, a new humanity is created, walls of separation are broken down, lost harmony is restored. Paul is particularly concerned with the separation between humanity and God, but sees this reflected in all the other divisions in human society, especially the division between Jew and Gentile. But he is also concerned with other separations, particularly those associated with gender, status and class.

There are numerous passages we could look at to explore this, but to give you a flavour of what this session is about, let me quote just one. Writing to the Christians in Corinth, and speaking about the new life we have in Christ, Paul says this:

> From now on, therefore, we regard no one from a human point of view; even though we once knew Christ from a human point of view, we know him no longer in that way. So if anyone is in Christ, there is a new creation: everything old has passed away; see, everything has become new! (2 Corinthians 5.16–17)

The second chapter of the letter to the Ephesians also develops this theme in beautiful and moving detail: it speaks of Christ creating 'in himself one new humanity' (Ephesians 2.15).

This compelling and life-changing idea, that we are redeemed in Christ, are recreated and made new, reaches another climax with particular reference to gender in those famous verses from the letter to the Galatians that will be at the heart of this session. Sometimes those who resist the idea that women and men can serve equally in the Church suggest that these verses only refer to baptism. Paul's primary focus is baptism. But he sees this as the fount of everything else. If the primary theme of this reading is the breaking down of barriers, then we should not put a barrier around baptism. Ministry flows out of our baptismal identity and cannot be separated from it.

As you read this passage, think of its astonishing significance for the whole of life. Because of what God has done in Christ, we no longer view each other from the perspective of difference but from unity. As we shall see, the freedom and the new humanity that is our baptismal identity flow into everything, including ministry.

Bible study: Galatians 3.26–29

[26]for in Christ Jesus you are all children of God through faith. [27]As many of you as were baptized into Christ have clothed yourselves with Christ. [28]There is no longer Jew or Greek, there is no longer slave or free, there is no longer male and female; for all of you are one in Christ Jesus. [29]And if you belong to Christ, then you are Abraham's offspring, heirs according to the promise.

Reflection together

- Read the passage a second time with different voices, perhaps reading a verse each.

- Invite everyone to say aloud a word or phrase that strikes them.

- Read the passage a third time.

- Share together what this word or phrase might mean and what questions it raises.

- Share together your own experiences of the Church. Have you found it a place of acceptance for different people?

Notes on some details of the passage

This passage falls right in the middle of Paul's defence of justification by faith in Galatians, in which he argues that it is nonsense to insist on people being circumcised in order to join the Christian community, since it is faith, not the law, that makes them God's children.

The inclusion of these three pairings of words – Gentile/Jew; slave/free; male/female – may well refer back to a Jewish prayer of thanksgiving, prayed by Jewish men each morning. In this thanksgiving the men gave thanks that they were not a Gentile, a slave or a woman, which would have barred them from various religious privileges.

The odd feature of this passage is that the first two pairings are joined by 'and not' – so literally it reads 'there is not Jew and not Gentile; there is not slave and not free'. The third pairing is different and reads 'there is not male *and* female'. The question is why Paul has changed this here. One possibility is that he isn't talking about gender at all but about marriage, since 'male and female' is a phrase often used to describe marriage. But given the prayer of thanksgiving and the reference to women there, the change is more likely to be a reference back to Genesis 1.26 and a further reminder that humanity, male and female, are created in God's image.

The gender agenda

The debate about women in ordained ministry is sometimes clumsily caricatured as a stand-off between liberal Christians who are prepared to twist Scripture in order to fit in with a gender-inclusive culture, and conservative Christians who remain faithful to the plain meaning of the text. This 'plain meaning', as we shall see later in this book, is focused on one or two passages. Clearly they have to be addressed, since they seem to prohibit women's ministry. But we wish to argue something else. Far from twisting or revising Scripture, those of us who believe that women and men should serve equally do so because Scripture demands it. However, Scripture – and this may seem a difficult point to grasp at first – is not read in a vacuum. In this respect, there may be no such thing as 'the plain meaning of the text'. Rather, the way we read and interpret the text is always influenced by the culture we live in and the different questions we bring. Therefore some texts that plainly mean one thing to one generation can and do mean something else to another. This doesn't mean that the meaning itself changes, rather that the Holy Spirit enables us to draw out new truths as we encounter new challenges.

This passage from Paul's letter to the Galatians is a very good example of how this works. In fact you can see it happening in the pages of the New Testament itself.

The first Christians begin from the standpoint that what God had done for them in Christ was for them as Jews, and it takes them a while to realize it is for everyone. Even then it is only after the Church is scattered following Stephen's martyrdom that anyone actively seeks to convert Gentiles – that is, anyone who isn't a Jew – to the way of Christ. In Antioch, which, incidentally, is the first place that the followers of Jesus are called Christians, some unnamed disciples from Cyprus and Cyrene speak to some Greeks about Jesus (see Acts 11.20). This is one of the most significant moments in the whole of church history. It is the practical outworking of what Paul means when he said that 'in Christ there is no Jew or Greek'. If the gospel of Jesus Christ belongs to everybody, then it must be proclaimed to everybody. But this leads to other uncomfortable questions: should a newly converted Gentile Christian have to be circumcised before being baptized? Is it necessary to receive the mark of the Law of Moses before receiving the mark of Christ?

This debate may seem odd and obvious to us today, but it wasn't for the first Christians. They were still trying to work out what a non-Jewish Christianity looked like. Eventually the Church met in Jerusalem – you can read about this in Acts 15 – and came to the decision that no additional burdens should be placed on Gentile converts. Baptism was sufficient in itself. Without this decision, Christianity may well have remained a Jewish sect and never become the worldwide faith it is today.

This is the first great example of the way our understanding of the revelation of the new and redeemed humanity we have in Christ is refined in the fire of the questions different cultures pose. It also shows how growth in the understanding of our faith often comes about through mission. It was the active sharing of the faith that led to a deeper understanding. But because we can read about this development in Scripture itself, it is particularly helpful when we face other, similar questions today.

As the early Church comes to its momentous decision that baptism belongs to everyone, and that Jews and Gentiles are equal in Christ, so that equality – the redeemed humanity we have in Christ – flows into every aspect of the Church's life, including its ministry. It wasn't that Jews and Gentiles were baptized, while only Jewish Christians had authority to teach and lead. Baptism was the entry point into the whole Christian life. Therefore this way of reading Scripture, and letting it interact with the different cultures we encounter, is it itself *biblical*.

It also goes some way towards explaining why it took another 1,800 years to work out what it meant to say there was no slave or free. For centuries, faithful Christians read the Bible and simply accepted slavery as a norm. But in the nineteenth century the great movement for re-form that led to the abolition of slavery was asking new questions. This in turn led Christian people back to the Bible and to a fuller acceptance of what Paul was teaching. They read the Bible with fresh eyes and discovered what had always been there but was hitherto unseen: that in Christ there is no slave or free. This did not happen without passion-ate debate about the texts of Scripture. It is sobering today to read the arguments produced by Christians defending slavery or defending the practice of apartheid on the basis of biblical texts.

In our day we now face the full implications of what it means to say there is no male or female. We have long since accepted this with re-gard to baptism, but we have not accepted its full outworking in the ministry of the Church. Our culture poses hard questions, and – as it has done for generations before us and our first forebears in the faith – compels us back to the Bible to look at this passage afresh and see how it is foundational for our life in Christ and must, therefore, influence all gender relationships, and with it the place of women alongside men in the leadership, teaching and sacramental ministry of the Church. But we are not contemplating this change in order to fit in with the culture (there are many things about our culture today that the Bible compels us to oppose and denounce). But it is the questions our culture poses that have facilitated a fresh appraisal of the place of women in the Bible, and led us to understand that women and men serving equally is not something new but a rediscovery in our day of what has always been there.

To ordain women into the ministry of the Church is, therefore, a legitimate development, fully consistent with Scripture. To say otherwise requires us to make two assumptions that for some are completely incompatible with Scripture and tradition, namely that the ordained priest's relation to the priesthood of Christ is different in kind from that of any other baptized person; and that a baptized woman's relation to Christ's priesthood is different from a baptized man's. The early Church taught that the 'unassumed is unhealed'; that is, that in order to save and heal the whole of humankind, Christ assumed *representative humanity*, not just maleness. Therefore just as baptism belongs to men and women, so must the priesthood and the episcopate. The ordination of women is a *revealing within our own culture of something that has always been present within the tradition*. In the very different, and inevitably male-dominated, culture that prevailed in biblical times, such a complete revelation was not possible. Nor has it been for much of the last 2,000 years, although more women have had leadership roles than people sometimes think. We can point to Abbesses such as Hilda of Whitby or Hildegard of Bingen, or the religious women in Essen and Quedlinburg who ruled their territories and answered only to the Pope.

In our day, the Holy Spirit, who always leads into truth, is helping us to see the decisive and climactic truth of this climactic passage: in Christ there is no male or female, all of humanity is redeemed in Christ, all of us belong to Christ and are heirs according to the promise. Because baptism belongs to all, so can ministry.

We 'are all children of God' says Paul (Galatians 3.26). Paul often uses the image of putting on new clothes to demonstrate the recovery of this truth and the difference baptism makes to life: he speaks of being 'clothed with a new self' (Colossians 3.12 and Ephesians 4.24), and in today's passage says that through baptism we have 'clothed ourselves with Christ' (Galatians 3.27). In other words, through what God has done in the death and resurrection of Christ, and because of our baptism into this dying and rising, we have put on – literally, 'been clothed' – with a new reality. Another famous passage concludes: 'Above all, clothe yourselves with love, which binds everything together in perfect harmony' (Colossians 3.14). And elsewhere he writes:

> Do you not know that all of us who have been baptized into Christ Jesus were baptized into his death? Therefore we have been buried with him by baptism into death, so that, just as Christ was raised from the dead by the glory of the Father, so we too might walk in newness of life. (Romans 6.3–4)

This harmony of the new and redeemed humanity is without division. The old categories of race, status and gender are subsumed into the new clothing that is Christ. We don't stop being Jews or Greeks or men or women, neither has status or class disappeared, although, thankfully, slavery is largely abolished. But the way we understand these categories changes forever, and a harmony and balance that was there in the creation (see, for instance, Genesis 1.27–28) is restored, or perhaps it would be more accurate to say recreated by the saving work of Christ. But reference to Genesis reminds us that this was what God always intended.

In another comparable passage, Paul says that 'you have stripped off the old self with its practices and have clothed yourselves with the new self, which is being renewed in knowledge according to the image of its creator' (Colossians 3.9–10). And we remember again that God created humanity male and female. 'In that renewal there is no longer Greek and Jew, circumcised and uncircumcised, barbarian, Scythian, slave and free; but Christ is all and in all!' (Colossians 3.11).

For discussion

In groups of two or three, ask people to share these questions:

1 Do you have any experiences of prejudice, not just in church
   but in any walk of life? Have you been ignored, belittled
   or mistreated because of gender or colour or any other
   characteristic that has caused people to exclude you?

2 Do you have any particular experiences of prejudice because
   of gender difference in the Church?

3 What is your experience of being accepted and included in
   the Church?

As a whole group:

4 How have you experienced Paul's vision of a new and
   redeemed humanity being lived out? What difference does
   this vision make to your understanding of the place of men
   and women in Church and society?

5 What excites you about Paul's vision? What further
   implications can you detect?

Going further

Paul's vision of the new and redeemed humanity we have in Christ
demands that we look with fresh eyes at the way we order the life of
the world and the Church and at the mutually supportive and complementary parts men and women play. This mutuality and complementarity is needed at every level and in every ministry.

Reflect for a few moments on how such a world and such a Church might look, and of the particular gifts, insights and experiences that the Church lacks by its exclusion of women from certain offices, particularly the episcopate.

Also reflect on the other barriers of separation that we are so good at constructing. What other constraints or exclusions might God be asking us to dismantle?

Finally, reflect on the idea of being clothed with Christ. What are the prejudices, misunderstandings and separations that God wants to address in your own life? And as you clothe yourself with Christ, what must also be stripped off?

Closing prayers

Pray with thanksgiving for the new and redeemed humanity we have in Christ.

Pray for those who are mistreated or excluded from church life because they are different in some way. Pray that the Church may reflect the harmony we see in Christ, and that we might find the courage to break down barriers of separation in ourselves and in the world around us.

3

The Women of the Early Church

Introduction

There is absolutely no doubt that women exercised a significant ministry in the Church in New Testament times. Mary, the mother of Jesus,
was the first to receive the good news brought by the angel (Luke
1.26–38). Women accompanied Jesus on his travels through Galilee,
supported him in his ministry (Luke 8.2–3), stayed with him at the cross
and were the first witnesses of the resurrection. Women were present
at the gatherings of the early Church after the resurrection and at the
day of Pentecost (Acts 1.14; 2.17).

Women also feature by name in many of the narratives about the early
Church. In the pages of Acts we meet Tabitha (9.36), Mary the mother
of John Mark (12.12), Lydia, whose house became the base for the
Church in Philippi (16.14), and Priscilla (also called Prisca), one of Paul's
close companions and collaborators.

In the letters of the New Testament we meet many women also by
name. Our passage for study this session is the last chapter of the letter
to the Romans. At one level it is a list of names and, you might think,
not very interesting. But look more closely. These are not just greet-
ings but commendations. See how many of those Paul is greeting are
women – and look carefully at the way they are described.

Bible study: Romans 16.1–16

1 I commend to you our sister Phoebe, a deacon of the church at Cenchreae, [2]so that you may welcome her in the Lord as is fitting for the saints, and help her in whatever she may require from you, for she has been a benefactor of many and of myself as well.

3 Greet Prisca and Aquila, who work with me in Christ Jesus, [4]and who risked their necks for my life, to whom not only I give thanks, but also all the churches of the Gentiles. [5]Greet also the church in their house. Greet my beloved Epaenetus, who was the first convert in Asia for Christ. [6]Greet Mary, who has worked very hard among you. [7]Greet Andronicus and Junia, my relatives who were in prison with me; they are prominent among the apostles, and they were in Christ before I was. [8]Greet Ampliatus, my beloved in the Lord. [9]Greet Urbanus, our co-worker in Christ, and my beloved Stachys. [10]Greet Apelles, who is approved in Christ. Greet those who belong to the family of Aristobulus. [11]Greet my relative Herodion. Greet those in the Lord who belong to the family of Narcissus. [12]Greet those workers in the Lord, Tryphaena and Tryphosa. Greet the beloved Persis, who has worked hard in the Lord. [13]Greet Rufus, chosen in the Lord; and greet his mother – a mother to me also. [14]Greet Asyncritus, Phlegon, Hermes, Patrobas, Hermas, and the brothers and sisters who are with them. [15]Greet Philologus, Julia, Nereus and his sister, and Olympas, and all the saints who are with them. [16]Greet one another with a holy kiss. All the churches of Christ greet you.

Reflection together

- Read the passage a second time with different voices, perhaps reading a verse each.

- Invite everyone to say aloud a word or phrase that strikes them.

- Read the passage a third time.

- Share together what this word or phrase might mean and what questions it raises.

- Make a list on a large sheet of paper of the women you meet in this passage and the ways they are described.

- As you look at the whole list, are you surprised or challenged or comforted by what you see?

- What questions would you ask these women in an interview?

Notes on some details of the passage

The final chapter of Romans indicates from the names mentioned that the epistle was written in Corinth. The way in which Phoebe is mentioned in 16.1 suggests that she took the letter to Rome, and some scholars believe she might even have been the one to read and interpret it to the Roman Christian community.

- The Greek word *diakonos* (here translated deacon in 16.1) was a common word in the Graeco-Roman world, and meant a servant (as opposed to a slave or *doulos*). It became used quite quickly in the early Church as a technical term to describe a 'minister' (as in Philippians 1.1), but it is hard to know what this role entailed in the New Testament period.

- The word *prostatis* (here translated as benefactor) is the word often rendered 'patron' in texts outside the New Testament, and refers to someone who has wealth that he or she uses to benefit those in the community. While 'benefactor' captures the generosity element, it doesn't quite communicate the high status of the person described like this.

- The question about Junia is whether she was a woman or not. If it is a man's name, the name would be Junias not Junia (to make it masculine). The problem is that while Junia is a very common name in the Roman Empire, Junias is entirely unknown. It is therefore very unlikely to be intended here as a man's name.

The ministry of women in first-century Rome

The letter to the Romans is written as Paul's letter of introduction to a church that was seen as important and influential among the earliest Christians. In the letter, Paul sets out the gospel he proclaims clearly and in some depth. He hopes to visit and to use Rome as a base for further mission work in Spain (15.22–24). In fact, as Acts tells us, he will be brought to Rome as a prisoner.

The number of women who feature in the list in Romans 16, and their roles, bear remarkable witness to the ministry of women in a key part of the life of the early Church. So does the fact that Paul takes this opportunity to lift them up, single them out and name them. Because the ministry of women has been contested over the years within the life of the Church, it is not surprising that this list has been translated into English in many different ways. If members of your group are using different translations, it will be worth comparing them as you work through the passage.

Phoebe has star billing in the list, probably as the bearer of the letter. She is given three titles: first of all, 'our sister' – a fellow Christian, child of God, fellow disciple on the Way; second, Phoebe is specifically described as a *diakonos*, a deacon, of the church in Cenchreae, the port of Corinth.

Deacon is a technical term and we need to pause for a moment here. The early Christians developed a new vocabulary for those who exercised ministry and leadership. There was no plan or instruction for this handed on by Jesus or by the twelve. The pattern emerged in different ways in different places, and different terms were used, at least initially. By the end of the New Testament period, the pattern and vocabulary had begun to settle.

The term deacon is one of the words that is found in the earliest traditions. It means 'servant' and therefore is sometimes translated 'minister' (the Latin word for servant). Some have argued that a deacon was a special sort of servant: one who was given authority and a commission to speak on behalf of someone else – an ambassador or emissary. To be a deacon was to share in a recognized ministry within the Christian community. The letter to the Philippians is addressed to 'those in Philippi with the bishops and deacons'.

Phoebe therefore holds a specific office to which she has been called and commissioned. This office seems to have developed out of the role filled by the seven appointed to serve in Acts 6, who not only undertook practical tasks on behalf of the community but who proclaimed the gospel. A list is given in 1 Timothy 3.8–11 of qualifications that had to be met before someone could serve in this office. The list is applied equally to women and men (3.11), and there is evidence outside the Scriptures for women filling this office as well as men in the early Church. Across the different traditions in the Church of England today it would not generally be contested that women should be ordained as deacons, even by those opposed to their ordination as priests or bishops.

Phoebe's third title is also interesting. Paul calls her a 'benefactor of many and of myself as well'. The Greek word is *prostatis*. The same root word is used in Romans 12.8, where the NRSV translation is 'the leader'. A range of meanings are possible, including leadership, administration and patron or helper of others. The combination of the three titles and Phoebe's role as the bearer of the letter indicate a person with a significant role in the Christian community, a role that goes beyond the local church at Cenchreae.

Prisca is the second person on the list, mentioned with her husband, Aquila, but here given pre-eminence in the order, as in a number of places in Acts. They are both named as Paul's co-workers, sharing presumably in every part of his ministry. They are commended, in an age where martyrdom was common, for risking their lives for the sake of the gospel. They too have a wider reputation and office than a single local church. It may be worth turning back at this point and reading the account in Acts 18.24–27 of the encounter of Priscilla and Aquila with Apollos in Ephesus. Priscilla and Aquila are seen correcting the theology and understanding of another gifted teacher – a striking role for a woman.

Mary is greeted as the next woman 'who has worked very hard for you'. This too would refer to Christian ministry, not – for example – manual labour to provide practical support. The next couple are also very interesting:

> Greet Andronicus and Junia, my relatives who were in prison with me; they are prominent among the apostles. (16.7)

As already noted, there has been debate down the years about whether Junia is a woman or a man, but the balance of evidence from ancient commentators onwards has been that she is a woman and that we have here another married couple. The most natural meaning of 'prominent among the apostles' is that they were accounted together as gifted witnesses of the resurrection of Jesus, like Mary Magdalene and the women who came to the tomb. Paul tells us they were Christians before him, which probably means that they were part of the very earliest church in Jerusalem.

There are more women later in the list. We read of Tryphaena and Tryphosa (16.12), who are 'workers in the Lord'. Paul greets the mother of Rufus, 'a mother to me also'. In the context of this list, this does not mean that Rufus' mother did Paul's ironing or cooked him the occasional meal. It means she ministered to him as a Christian, perhaps in his earliest days of the faith. He greets Julia and the sister of Nereus, about whom we know nothing further except that they are Christians of distinction within the Roman church at this time.

Once you've explored the evidence of the passage in some detail, stand back a bit and reflect on what this evidence means in the context of the whole of the New Testament. It does not mean, of course, on its own, that women should automatically be admitted as bishops in the Church of England today.

However, this detailed evidence of the role and ministry of women in the New Testament Church is vital for two reasons. First of all, it gives a very necessary context for the interpretation of the small number of passages in Paul's letters that appear to restrict the ministry of women very significantly, which will be our focus in the next chapter. In Romans 16, Paul is positive about the role and ministry of women, and specifically commends Phoebe and her contemporaries. This must provide the broader framework for the next part of the study.

Second, Romans 16 paints a vivid and lively picture of a church in which women and men minister together, where the gifts of all are cherished and valued, where there do not seem to be rigid distinctions or hierarchies. It is a picture faithful to the insight of Galatians 3, where there are no divisions on the grounds of gender. That too is a vital element in our own Church's discerning the way forward on the consecration of women as bishops in our own day.

For discussion

1 Ask each member of the group to make another list for themselves: a list of women who have ministered to them and with them in their Christian journey or whose ministry they have appreciated and valued.

2 Go round the group and ask each person to share two examples from the list and describe what they appreciate about their life and work.

3 Explore together the ways in which the evidence of women's ministry in Romans 16 confirms or adds to your picture of women and men in ministry in Genesis and Galatians.

4 How has the study of this chapter prepared you for looking together at the more challenging Pauline passages in the next section?

5 Are you more or less convinced than you were that it is right for women to be ordained as bishops in the Church of England at the present time?

6 What does the study of this passage have to say to the role of women in your own congregation in public worship, representative roles and in other ministries?

7 What is God saying to you today through this passage?

Going further

Here are three ways to reflect further on this passage and this session.

The first is thanksgiving and appreciation for the ministry of women. In this chapter of Romans, St Paul takes the lead in that particular ministry. Presumably he has no need to do so. Perhaps he is highlighting women's ministry alongside men's because there is some movement to undervalue that ministry developing in the Roman church. But as a man and as an apostle, Paul takes the time and the trouble to appreciate the ministries of a woman who is new to the community (Phoebe), and the women he has worked alongside in the past and who have ministered to him and with him.

So reflect for a few moments on the ways in which you give thanks and appreciate the ministry of women alongside men in the life of the Church and in society. How can you remember them before God with thanksgiving? How can you express your own thanks and appreciation for their ministries? One of the things Paul is doing in Romans 16 is setting a climate of appreciation within which a variety of ministries can thrive and grow. How can that happen within the life of your own church?

The second is our openness to receive the ministry of all within the body of Christ. The fact that so many ministries are commended here reminds us, because we need that commendation, that we are not always open to receiving help, support or leadership from a wide variety of people. Sometimes there are bars in people's minds formed by gender. Sometimes those bars are formed by race or colour, by sexual orientation or by past practice. Sometimes they are about class or educational achievement. Often the Church claims to be free of such prejudice, yet we discover in reality that ministry, leadership and roles of significance are offered only to a certain sort of person, despite obvious gifts and abilities of those beyond that group.

Take a good look at the local church you belong to. How are you fostering and cherishing the gifts of everyone and diversity in ministry? What might you need to change?

Finally, reflect for a moment on the three titles given to Phoebe. One, 'benefactor', perhaps refers to her natural gifts or, perhaps, to her wealth and position in society and the use she made of those. Another, 'deacon', refers to the ministry in which she was commissioned by the Church. But neither her gifts nor her position define her within the body of Christ. The most important title is the first one Paul uses: 'sister'. That title is precious because it describes her relationship both with her Lord as a child of one Father who is in heaven, and her relationship with Paul, with the community in Cenchreae, with everyone else on the list, with the church in Rome and with all of us.

The Christian family often have difficulty working out what God calls us to do and the right way to order our life together. As we shall see in the next chapter, that sometimes meant and means conflict and difference in the early Church and in our Church in the present day. But those conflicts and differences do not change the fundamental relationship men and women bear to one another within the Christian community. We remain sisters and brothers in Christ.

Closing prayers

Give thanks for and pray for all women who exercise ministry within the Church today and for the women of the past who have left a record of their deeds.

Pray for one another and for the whole Church as we wrestle together with decisions about future patterns of ministry and our common life.

Pray for the ministry of God's Church today, that we may see a full diversity of gifts and backgrounds.

4

Women, Teaching and Authority

Introduction

We now come to the three passages in the New Testament that are the most difficult to interpret! They are difficult to make sense of not because of the subject matter but for other reasons, as we shall see. Despite this, they are the passages that are frequently turned to as the ones of greatest importance in defining the role of women in the Church, in society and to some extent in the home.

This chapter is different from the others in this book in that it looks closely at the text of *three* separate passages. Its structure follows this, with two groups of questions and a shorter 'Going further' section.

Some of the debate about these passages has become very technical, and this has put some people off – can we really make sense of these passages in the Church today? We can, but only through careful reading.

Bible study: 1 Timothy 2.1–15

1 First of all, then, I urge that supplications, prayers, intercessions, and thanksgivings should be made for everyone, [2]for kings and all who are in high positions, so that we may lead a quiet and peaceable life in all godliness and dignity. [3]This is right and is acceptable in the sight of God our Saviour, [4]who desires everyone to be saved and to come to the knowledge of the truth. [5]For there is one God; there is also one mediator between God and humankind, Christ Jesus, himself human, [6]who gave himself a ransom for all – this was attested at the right time. [7]For this I was appointed a herald and an apostle (I am telling the truth, I am not lying), a teacher of the Gentiles in faith and truth.

8 I desire, then, that in every place the men should pray, lifting up holy hands without anger or argument; [9]also that the women should dress themselves modestly and decently in suitable clothing, not with their hair braided, or with gold, pearls, or expensive clothes, [10]but with good works, as is proper for women who profess reverence for God. [11]Let a woman learn in silence with full submission. [12]I permit no woman to teach or to have authority over a man; she is to keep silent. [13]For Adam was formed first, then Eve; [14]and Adam was not deceived, but the woman was deceived and became a transgressor. [15]Yet she will be saved through childbearing, provided they continue in faith and love and holiness, with modesty.

Reflection together

- Read the passage a second time with different voices, perhaps reading a verse each.

- Invite everyone to say aloud a word or phrase that strikes them.

- Read the passage a third time.

- Share together what this word or phrase might mean and what questions it raises.

- What does the passage suggest about the relative roles of men and women?

- What puzzles you about this passage? What questions would you like to ask of it?

- What do you need to know about the context of this passage in order to help you make sense of it?

Corrective concerns in Ephesus

Paul's pastoral letters to Timothy and Titus are often seen as later developments in which Paul is concerned about ordering a settled Church. In fact there is much more of a sense of crisis about this letter, where Paul is concerned to draw all the people of God back to apostolic teaching. We can see this in his opening remarks to Timothy in chapter 1: 'remain in Ephesus so that you may instruct certain people not to teach any different doctrine', that is, different from the apostolic heritage. And Paul's concerns continue to be outward looking rather than about purely internal matters. To be sure, there are instructions about who might or might not qualify for positions of responsibility (1 Timothy 3), and how to handle accusations of impropriety (1 Timothy 5.19–21). But there is little setting out the responsibilities of leaders, with the result that we in turn learn very little from the pastorals about what these roles would actually have involved.

Paul's concern in this passage is that we all live a 'quiet and peaceable life' (2.2) so that there would be no barriers to others coming to faith. This is the same concern he has expressed to the Christians living in Thessalonica (1 Thessalonians 4.11; 2 Thessalonians 3.12). He applies this principle in turn, first to men and then to women. So men, instead of being angry and arguing, should be focused on praying. 'Likewise' (v. 9), that is, for similar reasons and in a similar way, women should be less concerned with their appearance and more with holy living. Continuing this theme of appropriate behaviour, women are to learn in silence and full submission. It is striking that Paul is here encouraging women to learn, something that contemporary Jewish practice, and the Talmuds (Jewish teaching on the Law), at points explicitly prohibit ('Better to burn the Torah than teach it to a woman'; j. Sot. 3.19).

Paul is not here telling women to say nothing; if he were, he would have used a different Greek word (*sigao*, found for example in 1 Corinthians 14 and Luke 9.36). Instead, using the word *hesychios*, he is echoing the concern with which he began the chapter, that the women, like the men, should not be arguing or disputing but be listening carefully to the teaching they are being given. Nor does he say that women should be submitting to men here – their submission (like the men's) should be to the apostolic teaching.

The phrase 'I permit no woman' (v. 12) is an unusual one for Paul and suggests something specific to the context. But the main point of contention here is the meaning of the word translated as 'authority'. It is very unusual and occurs only here in the New Testament. In fact there are very few occurrences of it in Greek literature of the time. Where it does occur prior to the New Testament period, its sense is always highly negative, including a sense of 'murder'. It has the connotation of taking to oneself authority over the life of another, much as we would talk of 'taking someone's life'.

Paul's use of the creation order to emphasize women's sinfulness cannot easily be taken as an absolute statement since elsewhere in his writing he attributes the origin of sin to Adam without mentioning Eve (see Romans 5.14; 1 Corinthians 15.22). He might perhaps be correcting misunderstanding of his own teaching, but we also need to remember he is writing to Timothy in Ephesus, the home of the temple of Artemis. In Greek mythology, she was created first and only subsequently took a male consort, so there was a strong cultural assumption that women were both prior to and independent of men. Greek philosophy also suggested that the bodily was inferior to the spiritual, which would suggest that truly spiritual women should leave behind the mundane realities of motherhood. Against this, Paul strongly contests that the vocation of childbirth in no way disqualifies women from a full part in the story of salvation.

Putting textual and contextual facts together, it is difficult to read this passage as a permanent prohibition for every place on the teaching ministry of women. Paul's concern, in the context where people are drifting from the apostolic tradition, where women have been nurtured in a culture that suggests they are independent of men, and where they simply lack equal education, is that they should not be allowed to take on for themselves a teaching ministry that is not rooted in the teaching of the apostles. The following paraphrase tries to capture the thrust of what Paul is emphasizing.

It's really important, for the sake of the gospel, that we're not seen as troublemakers but as good citizens. Instead of causing problems with the authorities, we should be praying for them and playing our part in getting on with the daily business of life.

But we can't do this if we are constantly fighting with each other. So men, stop fighting, and get on with praying. Women, stop competing on how good you look and try competing on living well. I won't put up with any of you women setting yourselves up on your own authority and leading people away from the apostolic teaching. Instead, you should take your place along with everyone else as full members of the community of disciples, learning and growing in your faith.

Don't believe the myths around you that women are superior to men. Eve sinned just as much as Adam did! And don't believe that you have to give up on motherhood in order to be spiritual. Trusting in God, and growing in love and holiness, is as important for you as it is for everyone else.

For discussion

1   Do you think the way that your own congregation conducts its life commends the gospel to others or puts them off? What about at a national level?

2   How important do you see the teaching ministry within the Church? What does it mean for you as a congregation to be rooted in the apostolic tradition?

3   Do you accept the view that this passage cannot be read as a permanent prohibition on the teaching ministry of women?

Bible study: 1 Corinthians 11.2–16

2 I commend you because you remember me in everything and maintain the traditions just as I handed them on to you. ³But I want you to understand that Christ is the head of every man, and the husband is the head of his wife, and God is the head of Christ. ⁴Any man who prays or prophesies with something on his head disgraces his head, ⁵but any woman who prays or prophesies with her head unveiled disgraces her head – it is one and the same thing as having her head shaved. ⁶For if a woman will not veil herself, then she should cut off her hair; but if it is disgraceful for a woman to have her hair cut off or to be shaved, she should wear a veil. ⁷For a man ought not to have his head veiled, since he is the image and reflection of God; but woman is the reflection of man. ⁸Indeed, man was not made from woman, but woman from man. ⁹Neither was man created for the sake of woman, but woman for the sake of man. ¹⁰For this reason a woman ought to have a symbol of authority on her head, because of the angels. ¹¹Nevertheless, in the Lord woman is not independent of man or man independent of woman. ¹²For just as woman came from man, so man comes through woman; but all things come from God. ¹³Judge for yourselves: is it proper for a woman to pray to God with her head unveiled? ¹⁴Does not nature itself teach you that if a man wears long hair, it is degrading to him, ¹⁵but if a woman has long hair, it is her glory? For her hair is given to her for a covering. ¹⁶But if anyone is disposed to be contentious – we have no such custom, nor do the churches of God.

This is recognized as one of the most obscure passages in the New Testament – but we can still learn from it! There are difficulties about the text, questions about the context, and strange ways in which this passage has been used down the years. No one has yet offered a convincing explanation of the phrase 'because of the angels' in verse 10, or what it is that nature teaches us in verse 14. It is easy to forget that first-century understanding of the body, and the function of its parts, was very different from our understanding today. And perhaps most strangely, this passage has been used to defend the idea of women wearing hats. Whatever the shape of Paul's argument, his conclusion in verse 15 is that women have been given long hair *in place of* a head covering, so that a head covering (hat) is no longer necessary.

The most significant term in this passage is the word 'head', and there are three important things to note about it. First, verse 3 is the only place where Paul uses this word metaphorically. Everywhere else in the passage he is using it literally to refer to a part of the body. Second, the only place in the passage where 'authority' is linked with 'head' is in verse 10, and here it is about the woman exercising authority over her *own* head. (Some translations include the phrase 'a symbol of authority', but the Greek text that Paul wrote does not include the word 'symbol'.)

Third, we need to be aware of how hard we find it to let go of our own assumptions about what 'head' means. The 'head' teacher is the one in charge of the school; the 'head' of an army is the one who is in command; and the 'head' of the household is the one who exercises authority over other members. But this is not what Paul and his readers would have assumed. If you chop off someone's head, they do not go wild and out of control; rather, they drop down lifeless. So the natural assumption is that the head is not the thing that *controls* the body but the thing that *animates* it, that gives it life. Therefore the word 'head' in Greek did not have the primary metaphorical meaning of the one in control, having authority over, but of the one who gives life. We can see this in the language of the Old Testament. Where the Hebrew uses the word 'head' metaphorically to mean 'leader', the Greek translation rarely does, preferring to use a non-metaphorical term.

Paul's metaphorical use of 'head' in verse 3 supports this. If Paul had been thinking about authority, he would have put the players in a different order – God, Christ, man, woman. In fact he is pointing out that every man has his origin in Christ, the Creator; that, according to Genesis 2, woman has her origin in man; and that Christ himself had his origin in the godhead. He picks up this idea of origins explicitly in verse 8 but then subverts it in verses 11 and 12: woman might have come from man in creation, but every man since has in fact come from a woman. And since God is the origin of everything, including every gift and ministry in the body of Christ, then both men and women ought to be able to pray and prophesy in the assembly without causing offence. Women do not need to cover their heads, and should have a full part in the ministry of the local church. This, says Paul, is the universal practice of all the Christian congregations.

Bible study: 1 Corinthians 14.34–35

[34]women should be silent in the churches. For they are not permitted to speak, but should be subordinate, as the law also says. [35]If there is anything they desire to know, let them ask their husbands at home. For it is shameful for a woman to speak in church.

This is a very odd passage for several reasons. Three chapters further back in 1 Corinthians, as we have just seen, Paul has gone to great lengths to argue for women's praying and prophesying in the assembly.

So how can he now be telling them to remain silent? Paul consistently uses the language of submission not just of women to men but of all believers to all others. And nowhere else in his writings does he cite the law in this general way; he always refers to a particular passage. Some early manuscripts place these verses at the end of this chapter instead of here, and there is no evidence that any of the early church fathers were familiar with this passage. So it is clear that even the earliest generations of Christians had significant questions about this text.

Assuming that this *was* part of Paul's original letter, we need to read it in the context of what has gone before in his preceding three chapters. Paul is clear that the Spirit gives ministry gifts to both men and women and, as we have seen, he expects these gifts to be exercised. So perhaps the 'speaking' that he is prohibiting is the idle chatter of those who don't understand what is going on and are not used to taking a full part in the serious business of worship.

For discussion

1 What rules or practices in your own church would feel strange to a visitor from the past or the future?

2 How might we encourage every member of the congregation to exercise the gifts and ministry that the Spirit has given them? Are there groups and individuals who still feel as though they have little to contribute?

3 What guidelines do you have for participation in public worship in your own community? Should they be the same for men as for women?

Going further

The wider questions raised by these three passages transcend the specific issues of gender relations in the Church, and take us into the larger issues of how we read Scripture, the place of Scripture in the Church and how we handle disagreements.

The three passages are united by the serious difficulties we have in making sense of them, partly because of difficulties of vocabulary but also because we have lost that knowledge of the specific contexts that we would need to make full sense of what Paul is saying. For some reason, passages that are at the very margin of clarity have been placed centre stage in the debate about gender relations.

And what do we do with texts of Scripture that appear to be pulling in different directions? When one text appears to encourage women to speak out and yet a few verses later it seems to say the opposite? One approach in this discussion is to take a single verse or passage as the most important, and use this as a key to unlocking meaning in all other passages. The first problem with this is deciding which passage is the most important. It also carries the danger that passages no longer mean what they appear to mean – we can only make sense of them when they are shaped by the key passage we have previously settled on. This can make a nonsense of the original letters. How could the Corinthians interpret Paul's writing in the light of his letter to Timothy when that letter hadn't yet been written? Or was Paul's meaning in his earlier letters obscure until it reached its full flowering in his later writings?

A better approach is to read all these passages together, the straightforward and the challenging, taking into consideration both the specific context of each but also the shared concerns of all of them, and to see from this the shape of the scriptural message about women, men and ministry.

Reaching a consensus on the meaning of these passages within the Church is going to require further hard work, alongside honesty and integrity in the way we handle the information we have before us. In the meantime, there are plenty of things we can be confident about. First, mission matters. Second, how we relate to one another can help or hinder the process of others coming to faith. Third, the Spirit gives gifts to all as the Spirit chooses, and we need to go out of our way to enable the ministry of those who would otherwise be marginalized.

Closing prayers

Give thanks for the gifts that the Spirit has given you, and pray for courage to exercise this ministry faithfully.

Pray for relationships between members of your congregation and in the wider Church, that our love and concern for one another might draw others to experience for themselves the love of God in Christ.

Pray for those with particular teaching ministries in the Church, that God may guard them and use them to build up the whole Church in faith and in wisdom.

5

Women and Men in Family Life

Introduction

The Scriptures give us a variety of different models of men and women in family life, many of which are based around the concept of a household unit. This is a broad concept in both the Old and the New Testaments, reflecting economic and social expectations, as well as ordering personal relationships: between women and men (Genesis 2.24), between young and old (Psalm 78) and between parents and children (Colossians 3.20).

Both women and men are seen to lead such households (Proverbs 31.10 and 15) and are respected for their roles in the domestic and public spheres. In the pages of Acts we learn of a woman named Lydia who worked as a trader of fine cloth, whose household is baptized and who then hosts in that household one of the emerging churches (16.14, 15).

Recent discussion of the role of women and men in church leadership has often returned to selective biblical passages, particularly Ephesians 5, to argue that men and women have a fundamentally different place in family life, and that women are therefore limited in the roles they may take on in the Church.

We will examine this passage closely to understand more clearly the concept of mutual submission in Christ and the radical call to love, faithfulness and respect that is made to all Christians, male and female, as we further the mission of the Church.

Bible study: Ephesians 5.15–33

15 Be careful then how you live, not as unwise people but as wise, [16]making the most of the time, because the days are evil. [17]So do not be foolish, but understand what the will of the Lord is. [18]Do not get drunk with wine, for that is debauchery; but be filled with the Spirit, [19]as you sing psalms and hymns and spiritual songs among yourselves, singing and making melody to the Lord in your hearts, [20]giving thanks to God the Father at all times and for everything in the name of our Lord Jesus Christ.

21 Be subject to one another out of reverence for Christ.

22 Wives, be subject to your husbands as you are to the Lord. [23]For the husband is the head of the wife just as Christ is the head of the church, the body of which he is the Saviour. [24]Just as the church is subject to Christ, so also wives ought to be, in everything, to their husbands.

25 Husbands, love your wives, just as Christ loved the church and gave himself up for her, [26]in order to make her holy by cleansing her with the washing of water by the word, [27]so as to present the church to himself in splendour, without a spot or wrinkle or anything of the kind – yes, so that she may be holy and without blemish. [28]In the same way, husbands should love their wives as they do their own bodies. He who loves his wife loves himself. [29]For no one ever hates his own body, but he nourishes and tenderly cares for it, just as Christ does for the church, [30]because

we are members of his body. [31]'For this reason a man will leave his father and mother and be joined to his wife, and the two will become one flesh.' [32]This is a great mystery, and I am applying it to Christ and the church. [33]Each of you, however, should love his wife as himself, and a wife should respect her husband.

Reflection together

- Read the passage a second time with different voices, perhaps reading a verse each.

- Invite everyone to say aloud a word or phrase that strikes them.

- Read the passage a third time.

- Share together what this word or phrase might mean and what questions it raises.

- What does a *household* look like where people are faithful to God, subject to one another out of reverence for Christ and filled with the Spirit?

- What does a *church* look like where people are faithful to God, subject to one another out of reverence to Christ and filled with the Spirit?

- Which attributes would you like to ask God to develop in your own life, in both the domestic and the public spheres?

Notes on some details of the passage

This passage comes from the second half of Ephesians. Whereas the first half concentrates on the question of what God has done for the Ephesians, the second half reflects on what this means about how they should live. Ephesians 5 comes in a longish section (4.1—6.20) in which the question of how the Ephesians should live as Christians is explored in more depth. This particular passage is often called a 'household code', and it refers to how households – which in this context includes the wider family, servants and slaves – relate to each other.

- It is important to recognize that the Greek word used for women has the more specific meaning of wives (and likewise men/husbands). Many scholars accept that Paul's advice, here and elsewhere, is not general advice on women's attitude to all men but specific advice on how a wife relates to her husband.

- The word translated as 'be subject' is the Greek word *hupotassō*, which is hard to put into an English form that can be easily understood in today's world. In this context the verb probably has the sense of freely and willingly placing oneself in subject relationship, rather than being forced into it and rather than living a life in which one's own concerns are of more value than anyone else's.

- The word 'head' (*kephale*) is a metaphor, and this one is drawn from Paul's language about being the body of Christ, which he uses extensively throughout his writing. One of the key issues about metaphors is that we are meant to wrestle to work out what they mean. Although some think 'head' clearly means 'to have authority', it is by no means clear that it *can* mean this in a context in which everyone has subjected themselves to one another (5.21). Other options include the head being the 'source' or the 'public face' of the body.

Women and men in family life

We need to start by looking backwards. Ephesians 5 begins with a word, 'therefore', that takes us back to the previous chapter. It's vital that we hear the author's words in Ephesians 5 about renouncing fornication, impurity and greed, and submitting to one another in a Christian household, in the light of the earlier description in Ephesians 4 of a new way of living. Do not live as the Gentiles live, in the futility of their minds, abandoned to licentiousness, greedy to practise every kind of impurity, the author warns there, but live instead in goodness and forgiveness.

The author of Ephesians is trying to set out a distinctively Christian way of living in community. Although usually referred to as the Epistle to the Ephesians, in its earliest forms the letter is missing the description 'in Epheso' ('to the Ephesians'). It also lacks the signs of familiarity that Paul's other letters show with the communities to which they are addressed. If we were to see the epistle instead as a kind of circular letter, to a network of churches in a region, perhaps centred on Ephesus, we might appreciate more clearly its growing sense of the wider concept of Church, not just as individual communities but as an organic whole. As the body of Christ, all Christians are united and need to order their behaviour around the idea of submission to Christ, who is their author and their head.

Since a community's beliefs are bound to be judged by the lifestyles of its members, the author wants to set out a distinctively Christian way of living. This needs to be as authentic in the private sphere as it is in the public. And so a moral code is developed that concentrates on avoiding foolishness and drunkenness (and those deeds that are described as too shameful even to mention), and cultivating instead habits of prayerfulness, praise and thanksgiving.

Family life receives the most detailed treatment as the place where private and public roles come together. It is important to see that this section starts with verse 21, 'Be subject to one another out of reverence for Christ', and that this verse provides the verb 'subject' that is implied, although not actually repeated in the Greek, in the following verses. All Christians are called to submit to one another, following the pattern of Christ submitting, in loving intimacy, to God.

We should pause for a moment to examine the Greek word *kephale* in verse 22, which is often translated as 'head'. Note that this is not the same as 'leader', and does not imply authority in the same way that the Greek word *arche*, used elsewhere in the New Testament, could have done. Instead, the husband is metaphorically the head of the wife, just as Christ is the head of the Church, more in the sense of being the author or the source of life. 'The head of a river' is a modern metaphor that picks up the same meaning. The husband, like Christ, is to act in a sacrificial and loving way that brings life to the body of which he is the head, and with which he has become one flesh.

It is true that the relationship between women and men is not described in parallel terms in this passage. Verse 21 demands of men and women submission to their wives and husbands in the same way that it demands submission to and from everyone in the community out of reverence for Christ. The passage then repeats this injunction for wives in relation to their husbands, adding for husbands the extra responsibility of loving their wives (and not, by implication, other women). Given a context of marital breakdown, which brought particular vulnerability to women both because of their lack of legal status and because of their greater responsibility for the physical aspects of child-bearing and child-raising, the author of this pastoral letter is demanding a particularly high degree of respect and care for women. But he is doing so within a framework of mutual respect, love and submission that mirrors the equal, intimate and unbroken relationship between the Son and the Father.

Remember the 'therefore' with which Ephesians 5 begins. Christian communities are called to grow and develop around values that attest to their faith and that provide an attractive witness to those who are not yet convinced by the gospel. How this is to be done may vary in accordance with the social norms of the day. The author of this letter is certainly accommodating, in the communities he is addressing, Greek notions of male as head and female as body, rather than the Jewish norm of matriarchal power in the home and family. But whatever the cultural variation in actual roles and in the localized metaphors used to describe them, the fundamental values expressed here are about mutual submission in Christ, for the sake of creating a distinctively Christian identity based on goodness and forgiveness.

Family life has changed immeasurably since first-century Christians were trying to work out for themselves a new way of living under the authority of Christ. Developments in politics, medicine and law have brought about greater freedom than existed previously for women to operate as equals in the public sphere, and for men to flourish in their domestic roles. More people live in single-person households than ever before, and homosexual couples continue to challenge society to recognize a different but equal pattern of stable, loving and committed relationships. Although there are divergent views within the Christian community on the appropriateness of all of these developments, Christianity has, from its earliest days, undoubtedly played a part in developing women as bearers of the gospel message and leaders of God's households, in both familial and more public arenas.

We will therefore need to take a step back before we draw parallels between the roles of men and women in family life in the Ephesian communities and in our own cultural context. We will also need to be cautious in drawing any theological conclusions from this passage about the ordering of Christian family life and therefore the place of women in the Church. Although there is some accommodation to specific cultural situations in both Ephesians and other epistles (1 Timothy

2.8–15; 1 Corinthians 11.1–16) that appear to limit the role of women in both family and church life, the overarching direction of early Christian thinking is towards women having an equal role, both individually and alongside their husbands, in spreading the good news of Jesus Christ (Acts 9.36, 16.14, 18.24–27; Romans 16.1–15). The examples of women and men in early Christian life give us no reason to think that these changes should not continue in our own time with the further development of women's ministry as teachers and leaders in the Church today.

Throughout the descriptions of the earliest Christians, we see a radical and primary principle of equality emerging (Galatians 3.28). We also see the Church adapting in local situations in order to be fit for mission, developing a distinctively Christian way of living and offering the best witness it can in terms of both the private and public lives of its believers. Women and men have an equal part to play in both these spheres, furthering the mission of the emerging Church.

For discussion

1 Note how you feel when you read the description of Christ's sacrifice for his beloved children as a fragrant offering, observing that God gives us not just the bare minimum but an abundance of love. Reflect on how this might set the tone for the moral teaching that follows about individual, family and community relationships.

2 Go round the group and think of different examples of what it means for all people to submit to one another out of reverence for Christ. Can these examples apply equally to men and women?

3 Look together at the passage in Ephesians 5.21–33 where

male and female responsibilities in family life are described differently. How much are these role differences about fundamental values and expectations and how much are they about gender in family life being seen through the lens of a particular culture?

4 How might your Church need to adapt in our own culture in order to proclaim the gospel afresh for new generations?

5 What would you say to a victim of domestic violence whose spouse had argued that the Bible justifies submission?

Going further

You belong in this church family. Whether you are male, female or transgender, married or single, gay or straight, whether your own experience of family life is a good one or whether love and respect have been in short supply, you belong now in the Christian family. You can expect others within this family to put your best interests at heart, just as you will want to put their best interests at heart. As, like the rest of us, you are not perfect, although still dearly loved, you will need to be forgiven and, of course, to forgive. There is no place in this household for abuse or coercion: we love each other following the sacrificial example of Jesus Christ. You will want to live your life with us in a way that gives honour to God and demonstrates that Christ is our head and the source of our life.

It is no coincidence that Ephesians 5 moves into its discussion of family life from a description of praying, singing and making music. Worshipping together as God's household requires attentiveness and sensitivity. However good we may believe our individual voices to be, star performers are rarely required in either collective worship or in family life. Instead of seeking a prominent role, we are required to submit to each other so that the song we sing together convinces others that ours is a faith worth living.

You might want to ask yourself how you will live out this knowledge in your own life of faith. How will you give up some of your own needs in order to play a fuller part in the wider household of God? How will you accept the wisdom of others when you cannot see the full picture on your own? How will you cherish and protect those in your household and church family who are most vulnerable at any point? How will you be clear about the commitment you have made to those who are closest to you, a commitment that entails closing down the option of certain kinds of intimate relationships with others?

In our wider church life we will also want to reflect on the commitment that exists to our brothers and sisters in Christ. This may include following a call to serve in communities and parts of the Church where it seems difficult for the gospel to take root at the moment. It should include giving generously and wholeheartedly of our financial resources, to support churches that are part of the body of Christ even if we don't share their exact theological outlook. Our Church is not diminished by supporting others who see things differently from us. We do not lose personhood by acknowledging our need to submit to God and to each other; rather, we gain it.

As we see the earliest churches doing, we will want to hold fast to the gospel's primary value of loving inclusion, as well as organizing ourselves as effectively as we can for mission. This must involve women and men submitting to Christ, living lives that point attractively to gospel values, confidently leading the Church in its public ministry.

Closing prayers

Pray for all who are entering into faithful, committed relationships, asking that they will find ways of expressing respect and love to each other, submitting to each other out of reverence for Christ.

Pray for those who have been subject to violence in their families and especially for homes where the Bible has been misinterpreted as justifying these actions.

Pray for the ministry of the Church today that we may see women and men flourish as leaders of God's households, witnessing to the love of Christ in our own culture.

6

Women and Men in Ministry Today

Introduction

Women and men have always worked collaboratively in Christian ministry. As we have seen, Jesus had male and female followers who travelled with him supporting his ministry (Luke 6.12–16; 8.1–3). He taught both men and women (Luke 10.38–42), healed them (Mark 8.22–26; Luke 8.42b–48) and commended both women and men for their faith (Matthew 8.5–13; 15.21–28). Male and female followers witnessed his death, attended his burial (Luke 23.49–56) and spoke with him after his resurrection (Matthew 28.1–10; Luke 24.36–49).

The message of God's kingdom, which Jesus reveals, extends loving acceptance to women and men alike, regardless of age, social standing, ethnicity or cultural background. The Holy Spirit continued this work in the first Christian communities, where this same grace welcomed and united men and women in ministry as the body of Christ.

In our final study we will look at the body of Christ described in chapter 12 of Paul's letter to the Romans, to consider what Christian ministry might look like today. As you read about the members of Christ's body and the various gifts, you might ask: Is this list complete? Are other gifts needed in ministry today? In the examples Paul gives, it is worth remembering that none are based on gender.

Bible study: Romans 12.1–10

[1]I appeal to you therefore, brothers and sisters, by the mercies of God, to present your bodies as a living sacrifice, holy and acceptable to God, which is your spiritual worship. [2]Do not be conformed to this world, but be transformed by the renewing of your minds, so that you may discern what is the will of God – what is good and acceptable and perfect.

3 For by the grace given to me I say to everyone among you not to think of yourself more highly than you ought to think, but to think with sober judgement, each according to the measure of faith that God has assigned. [4]For as in one body we have many members, and not all the members have the same function, [5]so we, who are many, are one body in Christ, and individually we are members one of another. [6]We have gifts that differ according to the grace given to us: prophecy, in proportion to faith; [7]ministry, in ministering; the teacher, in teaching; [8]the exhorter, in exhortation; the giver, in generosity; the leader, in diligence; the compassionate, in cheerfulness.

9 Let love be genuine; hate what is evil, hold fast to what is good; [10]love one another with mutual affection; outdo one another in showing honour.

Reflection together

- Read the passage a second time with different voices, perhaps reading two or more verses each.

- Invite everyone to say aloud a word or phrase that strikes them.

- Read the passage a third time.

- Share together which ministry, gift or phrase has special meaning or raises questions.

- Make a list on a large sheet of paper of the ministries and gifts you find in the passage; consider the character that might be needed.

- As you look at the reading, what surprises or challenges do you find?

- Which ministries or gifts are needed today? Are there others needed?

Notes on some details of the passage

Romans 12 stands at a crucial place in the letter to the Romans. In Romans 1—11 Paul has been laying out the major pillars of what he believes about Christ and what Christ came to do. In Romans 12—16 he moves on to talk about what difference this all makes to how people live as Christians. Some think that verses 1–2 act as a summary for the whole of Romans 12—16.

- It is important to notice the interweaving various themes in verses 1–2. Especially important is the bringing together of presenting our bodies to God with spiritual worship and the renewing of our minds. The correct response to God's mercy therefore involves the whole of who you are.

- The word translated 'spiritual' is in fact a rather odd word, *logikos*, from which we get our English word 'logical', and therefore means something like 'thought through worship'.

- The word for 'transformed' is the Greek word *metamorpheō*, which in the gospels is translated as 'transfigured'.

- Paul presents two kinds of 'gift lists' in his writings. Those that describe gifts to individuals (this one and 1 Corinthians 12.4–11) and those that describe gifts to the Church (1 Corinthians 12.27–28; Ephesians 4.11–12).

Women and men in ministry

Chapter 12 of Paul's letter to the Romans offers a clear and concise teaching on 'Being Christian'. For women and men in ministry today, the passage gives instruction on how God commissions ministry, builds relationships and transforms human character. Based on the personal greeting found in the letter's closing (Romans 16.1–16), as we have seen, Paul is writing to men and women actively engaged in Christian ministry.

Paul's teaching reminds early Christians – and us – that as we experience God's gracious love and compassion we are enabled to surrender our lives to him. This form of re-dedication – offering 'ourselves' completely to God – is the purest form of worship. Therefore serving God by submitting *our* will to *his* becomes a central part of our daily lives.

The spiritual transformation we experience in God (vv. 2–3) occurs 'by the renewing of your minds', which includes changing our behaviour and priorities. It is an ongoing process. Each day the Christian character of men and women, ordained and lay, is reshaped through prayer and Bible study, as well as personal encounters and daily experiences of life's circumstances. We learn to think, act and respond differently as the loving power of God forms us into the body of Christ.

We experience a shift in priorities – what *I* want to do as opposed to what *God* wants me to do – and we begin to view ministry, ourselves and others differently. The humbling process in verse 3 explains how we begin to think less of ourselves and more of others. For example, in the Church of England today, male priests who may have had difficulty working alongside ordained women come to recognize and appreciate those gifts previously exercised exclusively by their male peers now being demonstrated by their female counterparts. They accept the inclusive nature of God's grace. Likewise, women priests who experience the painful rejection of their gifts by their male peers or church parishioners are humbled as they learn prayerfully to forgive others. As women and men continue to grow by submitting themselves to God's 'renewing' work, collaborative ministry and diversity in the Church will thrive.

Paul describes brothers and sisters functioning harmoniously together as the body of Christ (vv. 4–5). This phrase, which symbolizes the interworkings of Christian ministry, occurs in other Pauline letters (see 1 Corinthians 10.16, 12.27; Ephesians 4.12). In considering the human body, we find that many of the members are arranged in sets of two – eyes, ears, arms, hands, legs, feet and so forth. Even the single nose has two nostrils, and the mouth has two lips. Consequently, the human body is a suitable metaphor to describe men and women joined collaboratively in Christian ministry. Just as the outer workings of the human body are easily seen by others, likewise male and female relationships in the

Church – how they work or don't work well together – are scrutinized by those we are trying to reach in our parish communities, schools and businesses.

In Paul's analogy, the various members of the body function as a single entity in Christ, with each part intricately connected to the other as all members are 'one of another'. Consequently, when one member – male or female – is missing or obstructed from functioning, the body is encumbered.

The point is clear. Different members have different functions, and the gifts each member contributes vary to reveal the diversity and inter-dependency essential to successful Christian ministry. The work of Christ's body is not limited to a select group of specially gifted people; rather, all members have an important role to play in support of a common mission.

To accomplish this mission, God releases gifts, or *charismata*, to the Church (vv. 6–7); the gifts are given according to the grace, or *charis*, of each member. The Greek word *charis* also translates as 'blessing' or 'divine presence'. This means that the gifts God gives are intended to bless his Church. Irrespective of gender, God entrusts the gifts to individuals he chooses (1 Corinthians 12.11), commissioning their use in ways that promote increase and unity in his kingdom (1 Corinthians 12).

A cautious reading of verses 6–8 is needed as the list of gifts is not exhaustive. A similar grouping appears in Paul's first letter to the Corinthians and may be read for comparison. Paul's reasons for writing to the two churches differ, yet several parallels exist in the letters concerning spiritual gifts (1 Corinthians 12.4–11) and the body of Christ (1 Corinthians 12.12–27).

Further care is needed to avoid taking these passages to mean that some Christians have gifts while others have none. A more conscientious reading of Paul's teaching is that different people have different gifts. Every Christian doesn't have the gift of preaching or teaching or leading; nor is every gifted musician an equally talented singer or composer.

For women and men in Christian ministry, the passage ensures that with such a rich array of spiritual gifts, every member of the body has a purpose and function to perform. No gift is negligible and all gifts are needed; there are no inferior gifts and no superior blessings. And because gender is conspicuously absent from this teaching on ministry, we can conclude that the gifts and their complementary functions are interchangeable. In other words, Christian ministry flourishes when women and men exercise their God-given gifts in order to bless his Church.

In verses 9–10 Paul explains how this is made possible – love. Paul's teaching on love in 1 Corinthians 13 may be more familiar, as it is often read during Christian weddings. However, the love he describes here and in 1 Corinthians is the Christian love shared between members of the body of Christ.

In verse 9a Paul's statement is emphatic and most Bible translations fail to capture his passion – genuine love is not hypocritical! The Greek word *agape* refers to the godly love shared between Christians. *Agape* is the selfless love demonstrated by Christ on the cross and memorialized in the Eucharistic meal. It is an altruistic love enabling Christians to discern and receive God's blessings to the Church while putting aside personal preferences or desires. Alternatively, when our actions deliberately hinder or dispose of those blessings God intended to benefit his Church, we are opposing his will and acting hypocritically. No brother or sister exercising Christian *agape* knowingly circumvents God's blessings to others.

The following verses (9b–10) reveal the implications of *our* will being conformed to *God*'s will. There are visible outward manifestations of the internal transformation and renewal taking place within us. We see our differences put aside, mutual respect and affection increases, gifts offered are generously accepted and motivated to flourish, while ministries and churches thrive. Noticeably, members graciously offer the seat of honour to another.

Jesus' teaching in Luke's Gospel (14.7–11) describes the humility associated with Christ-like *agape*. A more contemporary illustration of Paul's teaching in verse 10 is given here:

> Imagine two Christians who happen to arrive at an exit door at approximately the same time. Rather than rushing ahead of one another, each one stops momentarily and graciously gives way, offering the other clear access to exit the building first.

Like Christ, we find that women and men in ministry willingly place the well-being of others first while considering themselves last.

For discussion

1 Make a list of church ministries where you have experienced traditional roles or functions interchanged between women and men. Discuss any challenges or benefits.

2 Have each member share at least two experiences – one from a woman and one from a man – that significantly influenced their life.

3 In groups of two or four, give each group an apple seed, blossom (if you can find some) and an apple sliced in quarters

or halves. Ask them to reflect on 'transformation and renewal' before discussing their thoughts (and eating the apple). Have each group openly share their responses.

4 Have all participants stand together forming a circle an arm's length apart. Using a small soft-play ball, have them toss the ball to one another. Each person catching the ball should toss it to someone else in turn. Next, have everyone hold one hand behind their back. Repeat the play. (Extend the exercise by having participants raise one leg while standing and continue tossing/catching the ball with one hand.) After, ask each person to describe their experience with one word. Then as a group discuss how excluding women or men from various ministries impacts church mission and growth.

5 What does this passage say to you about women and men in ministry today?

Going further

Here are ways to reflect further on this passage and this session.

First, offer thanksgiving to God for the ministry of women and men that you have experienced in your life. In your thanksgiving remember that God gives every gift to those he chooses – the decision is his. Thank him for his discernment in giving gifts to those we might otherwise overlook.

As you reflect, remember that as Christians we are called to accept the gifts God gives his Church. Are there members with certain gifts or ministries that you take for granted? Are there others you fail to appreciate? Thank God for the ministries and those sharing their gifts with you and his Church. Ask him to reveal ways in which you can exercise greater appreciation for the ministry of others.

Next, as you think about the ministries and gifts in your church, consider if there is a general openness that allows room for diversity. Do some ministries appear exclusive? Are others encouraged to share their gifts? Or do some ministries operate like a private social club? For example, perhaps the teas and coffees after the service are always prepared by women, or possibly only men take responsibility for care of the church grounds. While some functions may be considered traditional roles, prayerfully consider if this accurately models the body of Christ. Do you know women with 'green thumbs' or men with basic culinary skills?

In today's teaching the Apostle Paul omits assigning gender to the ministries and gifts God gives the Church. As you give thanks for the ministries in your church, ask him to remove any barriers that may prohibit others from exercising their gifts. Then ask him to make you and the Church receptive to the generous offerings of others and the rich diversity the body of Christ is called to exhibit.

Finally, in this chapter *agape* is described as selfless Christian love. Think about this type of love. How is it expressed in ministry between church members? Or to others? Do women and men work together harmoniously? Is pride present? Or does Christ-like humility prevail among members? When disagreements occur, are they settled graciously in ways that honour God? Take time here to pray for any special needs or difficulties currently taking place in the Church on issues of gender or diversity. Ask God to unite members and help them reconcile their differences in order to receive his blessings for the Church.

As you reflect on Christian love, remember that there should also be visible manifestations present in our parish communities, local schools and businesses. How is this happening in your church? What message does your church send to others? Generously accepting? Or rigid and closed-minded? Here focus on mission and remember that God gives ministries and gifts to the Church to support *his* purposes, not our own. In prayer take this opportunity to seek God's guidance in recognizing his mission for you, as well as your church, and thank him for all he has provided thus far.

And finally

As you come to the end of this series of Bible studies, look back and reflect on what you have learned together about women and men in Scripture.

How will you think differently about the questions facing the Church about women and the episcopate? What will you do individually and together about these issues in the future?

Closing prayers

Give thanks for and pray for all women and men who exercise ministry together in the Church today and for those in the past who have forged the path for others.

Pray for one another and for the whole Church as we wrestle together with decisions about future patterns of ministry and our common life.

Pray for the ministry of God's Church today, that we may see a full diversity of gifts and backgrounds.

The Story of the Recognition of the Ministry of Women in the Church of England

From churchwardens to Members of Synod: lay women in leadership

Progress towards the inclusion of women in the governance, leadership, mission and ministry of the Church has been slow and contested. In the nineteenth century Anglican women, including Florence Nightingale, Josephine Butler and Octavia Hill, were among the most significant social reformers, but not all of them were political reformers. Octavia Hill regretted the campaign for women's votes on the grounds that 'men and women help each other because they are different, have different gifts and different spheres, one is the complement of the other'.[1] This argument continues to be heard, and for many years meant that women could have no formal part in church debates.

In 1897, as the Church of England began to recognize the contribution of lay people to its leadership, Parochial Church Councils were created in the Canterbury Province of the Church of England 'to quicken the life and strengthen the work of the church'. The elected councillors were

---

1 Sean Gill, *Women and the Church of England*, SPCK, 1994, p. 207.

to be 'male communicants of the Church of England of full age'. Some 1,100 women petitioned the House of Bishops to be allowed to stand for election, and two bishops pointed out that there were already women churchwardens in their dioceses, who would be *ex officio* members of the new councils. But in the decisive debate in Convocation[2] the Archdeacon of Exeter argued that allowing women councillors would bring them near to 'the governing work of the church', and he saw a 'real danger lest the distinction between sex and sex should be forgotten'. It would be 16 more years before women were allowed to join PCCs.

In 1903 a National Church Council was formed, including lay people directly in the governance of the national Church for the first time. Women were again excluded from membership until after the Parliamentary Reform Act allowed them to become Members of Parliament and the Church looked as though it was getting left behind. Forty women were elected to the new church National Assembly in 1920. Among them were two women who typified the different ways their successors would work for the full inclusion of women in the Church. Maude Royden, gifted in both prayerfulness and intellectual rigour, sensed a vocation as a preacher. Thwarted in this she became a campaigner on and beyond the margins of the Church of England. Her successors included Dr Una Kroll who, sitting in the Church House balcony for a major debate in 1978 on a motion to bring forward legislation for the priesting of women, appropriated a biblical text in her anger, shouting, when the motion was narrowly lost, 'we asked for bread and you gave us a stone' (Matthew 7.9). Alongside Maude Royden sat Louise Creighton, widow of a former Bishop of London, who by contrast would continue to argue for change from within the establishment. Her successors included Dame Betty Ridley, who became Third Church Estates Commissioner in the 1970s, and Dame Christian Howard, whose General Synod background papers on the ordination

---

2 Canterbury Convocation (1987) 227 (Resolution 5).

of women to the priesthood[3] became the set texts for theological and legislative debate in the 1980s.

From parish workers to priests: bishops' authorization of women in ministry

In 1898 it was reported[4] that about half a million women were occupied more or less continuously in church work. Most worked without pay as the wives, daughters and sisters of clergy. In addition there were hundreds of thousands of Sunday School teachers and the members of the Mothers' Union and Girls' Friendly Society. Gradually women were gaining confidence and experience, and the revived women's religious orders and the Deaconess order offered a structure for spiritual and social work, particularly among those living in the terrible conditions of the fast expanding cities.

In the newly flourishing Missionary Societies, single women were barred from service. In the words of the Bishop of Calcutta, responding to the offer of a single woman's help in 1842: 'The whole thing is against the Apostolic maxim: "I suffer not a woman to speak in church."' But in the early twentieth century the Societies had changed their policies, and by 1909 the majority of CMS missionaries were female, working with women – particularly those living in purdah – and children, and increasingly in situations that called for initiative, bravery, determination and administrative ability that went some way beyond what would have been acceptable at home.

Meanwhile the status of women working in parishes remained unclear. In 1907 the Bishops commended the excellent work being done by the

---

3 GS 104, GS Misc 88 and GS Misc 198.
4 A. Burdett-Coutts (ed.), *Women's Mission*, London, 1893, p. 364.

Church Army mission women but agreed that it would 'not be expedient to give any such recognition to them as the adoption of a form of licence would imply'.[5] The order of Deaconess, revived in 1861, grew slowly, with debates about whether celibacy or community living were to be required. Subordination to the parish and to the priest certainly were required. But as the role became more established, new possibilities emerged. A suburban vicar wrote to the *Daily Mirror* in 1918 that 'the duties of a Deaconess are similar to those of a layman, who can act in all capacities but those of pronouncing absolution or administering the sacrament ... she can even baptize when there is no clergyman within call.'[6] However, after debates at Lambeth conferences in 1920 and 1930, the Anglican Communion rejected the idea that Deaconesses might be considered as clergy and prohibited Deaconesses from liturgical leadership.

But formal resolutions and agreements by the Anglican Communion were to be overtaken by events. On 27 January 1944, Bishop R. O. Hall of Hong Kong and South China wrote to two friends to tell them that on St Paul's Day 1944 he had ordained a Chinese woman in the Church of God. Florence Li Tim Oi had been in pastoral charge of a parish for four years and had received the same training as male clergy. In an isolated community, with no other clergy available, her bishop argued that – as with Cornelius – she had shown her charisma and her congregation should receive the sacraments. Li Tim Oi was able to function fully as a priest for 18 months. When news of her ordination reached Canterbury, her bishop was told to suspend her (which he refused to do), but Florence resigned, only resuming her priestly ministry in Canada in 1983. Meanwhile, the Lambeth Conference having agreed that there was no valid theological objection to the ordination of women to the priesthood, two further women were ordained priest

---

5 Quoted in Brian Heeney, *The Women's Movement in the Church of England 1850–1930*, Oxford University Press, 1988, pp. 57–8.
6 Heeney, p. 131.

in Hong Kong in 1971, to be followed by further ordinations around the Anglican Communion.

In England, women who held a Bishop's licence as Lay Workers or Deaconesses were asked by Dr Mary Tanner in 1976 about the work they were doing and how they came to be doing it. What struck her was 'how, against all the odds of upbringing, existing role models, of male patterns of ministry, often in the face of being told to go away, think again, by the parish priest, certainly without any fostering of vocation by the bishop or the clergy, these women became convinced of a call to minister to the church'. Mary noted vocations 'that grew slowly and painfully against all that was expected, wanted, hoped for … These women were aware that the community was calling forth gifts that they themselves were often not aware they had to offer.'[7]

In 1984 the General Synod again debated a motion that legislation to permit the ordination of women as priests should be brought forward. Ronald Bowlby, Bishop of Southwark, argued that 'the only way to safeguard the doctrine of God is to ordain women as well as men … Because the tradition, grounded in scripture is precisely that mankind, male and female, is made in the image of God and because, when Christ died and rose again from the dead, he redeemed all who believed in him, women as well as men, and incorporates them in his body, the Church, by baptism.' By the time legislation was prepared, the majority of the House of Bishops agreed, and – in its report on the legislation sent to the Dioceses – argued that the biblical passages the House had studied, from both the Old and New Testaments, were most concerned with asserting the equal status and dignity of men and women.[8] A digest of the report, including commentary on debated texts, was sent to Diocesan Synods in 1990 to equip members for the theological debate ahead.

---

7 Mary Tanner, *Towards a Theology of Vocation*, ACCM, 1986.
8 GS Misc 337.

In 1986 General Synod passed legislation to enable women to become Deacons and, after the ordinations in 1987, women in authorized ministry, most of them previously Deaconesses, became more visible. For the first time they wore clerical dress, carried the title 'Rev' and were authorized to take weddings.

The 'normalization' of women clergy, legislation that allowed parishes to vote to exclude women clergy, financial provision to those clergy opposed who decided to leave, as well as the educational and campaigning work of the Movement for the Ordination of Women, enabled the Measure to find approval in the Dioceses and in the General Synod (where a two-thirds majority was just achieved in the House of Laity). Many had expected the Measure to fail, and the House of Bishops was concerned that the Church would split. The Ecclesiastical Committee of Parliament was vocal in its support for those who could not accept women priests. An Act of Synod granting additional provisions, including the appointment of Provincial Episcopal Visitors, was passed in 1993 and gave formal assurance of the continuing place for those opposed. In 1994 the first women were ordained to the priesthood in the Church of England.

From incumbency to episcopacy: ordained women in leadership

By 2002 the total number of women clergy was 2,539, 20 per cent of the total clergy numbers. By 2005 half those being ordained priest were women and many were incumbents. In subsequent years significant numbers of women have been appointed Area Dean, Residentiary Canon and Archdeacon, and by 2012 there were four women Deans of Cathedrals. In 2004[9] over 80 per cent of clergy supported the ordin-

9 Ian Jones, *Women and Priesthood in the Church of England Ten Years On*, Church House Publishing, 2004.

ation of women, tension about the issue had eased and nearly 70 per cent of clergy and laity supported the consecration of women Bishops. But the debates about the authority of and interpretation of Scripture continued, and research flagged up this issue as being a flashpoint over which support for women bishops would be won or lost.[10]

By the time of writing in 2013, women have been consecrated to the Episcopate in six Provinces of the Anglican Communion (most recently Southern Africa), women have attended two Lambeth conferences as Bishops, Bishop Victoria Matthews has had oversight of Dioceses in Canada and is currently Bishop of the earthquake-devastated Christ Church, New Zealand, and the Presiding Bishop of the Episcopal Church is Katharine Jefferts Schori. Under current legislation the confirmations and ordinations by those Bishops are not recognized by the Church of England.

In England in 2000, the House of Bishops, at the request of General Synod, set up a working party focusing on the issues around women in the episcopate. Its weighty report, chaired by the Bishop of Rochester and published in 2004, includes significant discussion of the interpretation of Scripture, but the Reader's guide was brief and Rochester was more referred to than read. The Synod moved on to drafting and revising legislation. With strong support from Dioceses – and later from Members of Parliament – for women to be included in every level of ministry, and resistance to creating a 'church within a church', the sort of compromise struck in 1992 and 1993 was no longer possible, although provision for oversight of parishes by traditionalist bishops was included. The Measure put to the General Synod in November 2012 gained an overall majority of 75 per cent but failed to get the required two-thirds majority in the House of Laity. In January 2013 a new working party began to prepare the way for new legislation to be brought to General Synod for first consideration in July 2013.

---

10 Jones, p. 201.

Frequently Asked Questions

1 If we read the Bible in its original context, are we in danger of watering down the word of God? Shouldn't we just take it at face value and obey what it says?

All texts are produced in a particular time and place. Part of the meaning of a text is derived from the context in which it is issued. If I shout 'Fire!' standing in front of a line of soldiers holding guns, it will mean something different from my shouting 'Fire!' on discovering my waste-paper basket ablaze. The same word has different meanings and I would anticipate different actions to result from it. It's the same with the Bible.

Acknowledging the importance of context in reading the Bible, however, does not mean we have to know everything there is to know about the ancient world in order to read or understand it. The plain text *does* speak, and has done throughout history, but a fuller and richer reading is gained by taking into consideration the world in which it was written. If we don't do this, and simply take it out of context, it is possible to prove all sorts of ridiculous things about God and the way we live now. Oppressive regimes such as apartheid were justified by biblical stories taken out of context and used wrongly. The way to guard against this kind of misapplication of the Bible is to be aware of the situation in which the text was written and what it was originally intended to do.

We also need to recognize that we read the Bible in our *own* context and bring to our reading our own knowledge, presuppositions and agendas. In that sense, no reading of Scripture will ever be entirely objective, much as we might want to claim that. The Bible wasn't written in English, so our interpretation of the text depends also on the way we translate certain words, as the studies in this book have shown. We can try to be as accurate as we can about that task, using the most up-to-date scholarship and research, but in the end all translations, and therefore all interpretations, will be subjective to some extent or other.

Reading the text in context does more to honour and respect the Bible text, not less. It is taking it more seriously, not less. There is a positive value in wrestling with it to receive its blessings. Reading the Bible with a knowledge of the world in which it was written and taking that into account in its application does not deny that it is truth and the living word of God. Indeed, it comes most to life when we allow the worlds that lie behind these two contextual encounters – that of writer and reader – to collide and bring transformation to the way we live.

2 Can I believe in the authority of the Bible and also agree with the ministry of women at all levels of leadership in the Church?

Yes, you can. Some have argued that that 'taking the Bible seriously' demands an entirely literal reading that arrives at a 'complementarian' position of male headship in Church and family. Sadly, it is sometimes suggested by those who hold this view that people who promote gender equality are 'not living under the authority of Scripture'. Actually, there has developed such a weight of serious biblical scholarship behind the 'egalitarian' perspective from respected scholars, that such a view cannot be simply dismissed as 'unbiblical'. In fact if one takes seriously the authority of the Bible, it is not only *allowable* but *essential* to see women's ministry without restrictions as consonant with Scripture. It is my belief in the Bible as the word of God with complete authority in all matters of life and conduct that leads me to view the full participation of women in the Church's life as a Godly imperative.

The claim is sometimes made that an egalitarian view of women and men in Church is simply following a modern, liberal agenda, going with the prevailing mood, capitulating to a postmodern 'anything goes' culture. But this is not simply a human rights issue, and not even only an equality issue. The Bible has much more to say about self-sacrifice, humility and responsibility for the good of all than it does about self-promotion and 'rights'. However, when the whole, wide sweep of biblical witness about men and women is taken to account, together with the trajectory that affirms the restoration of male and female together in Christ in the redemption of the whole of creation (as has been shown in the chapters of this book), the affirmation of women as leaders becomes a compelling, thoroughly biblical vision.

3 If I agree with equality in leadership in the Church, does it automatically follow that I will be 'liberal' in other matters, such as human sexuality?

No, it doesn't. Some people suggest that affirming women's ministry will inevitably lead to a reassessment of prohibitions on homosexual relationships, for instance. Some, especially some Evangelicals, have lumped together women in leadership with homosexuality, stating that the one sets us on a slippery slope to the other, and that if we don't hold the line on women, we'll have no basis to do so with sexual ethics either. However, this is to fail to recognize that these issues, while sharing some common themes, are not exactly the same hermeneutically and must be individually examined. The question is how we handle cultural accommodation in relation to particular issues and by which principles we do so.

4 Can I hold to the biblical concept of headship in family life and marriage while believing something different about the Church?

Some would want to hold to there being a role for a male 'head' in a family (although noting that the term 'headship' itself does not appear in the Bible), while also accepting the full ministry of women in the Church, including as bishops.

'The husband is the head of the wife' and 'Men are the head of the Church' are different statements, representing different concepts. Sometimes they are wrongly considered to be two sides of the same coin, and therefore taken together as equally true. However, as the studies here on Ephesians 5 and 1 Corinthians 11 have shown, they are not the same thing at all. It does not necessarily follow that the patterning of the family should determine the patterning of the Church, and the biblical evidence for this argument is very weak. In Ephesians 5 the same word 'head' is used for two different relationships: Christ and the Church, and husband and wife.

At no point is any reference made to the respective roles of men and women in the Church or society more generally. Ephesians 5.23 does say that 'the husband is the head of the wife' (although as the chapter in this book points out, this needs to be subject to cultural interpretation). But nowhere does it say that 'the man is head of the Church'. That is too big a leap to make and is taking theology from one sphere (marriage) and applying it erroneously to another (gender and church order).

What happens, we might ask, if a woman becomes a bishop? Can her husband still be head in their marriage, while she is a leader in the Church? I think so. We are used to seeing ourselves in different patterns of authority in different spheres of our lives more generally and adapting the way we operate accordingly.

Whatever we consider 'the husband is the head of the wife' to mean in practice today, it is certainly true that he is to be her 'head' in the same way as Christ is the 'head' of the Church; not domineering or commanding, but nurturing her and laying down his own life for her sake. A husband who is this kind of loving 'head' will encourage his wife to reach the full potential of God's calling for her life, including, perhaps, as a church leader. I know several couples where the husband has given up his own job and moved to a new area to enable his wife to pursue a vocation to church leadership. These men are truly exercising this kind of loving 'headship'.

5 If women are meant to be leaders, why did Jesus choose 12 male disciples?

There are several reasons suggested for Jesus' choice. It is argued that to include women in his inner circle in those days would have been highly controversial socially, and that women were not seen to be reliable witnesses. However, Jesus did many other things that were culturally unacceptable, and he chose a woman as the first witness to his resurrection, so I'm not entirely convinced by that argument. There is also the view that he chose 12 free Jewish males to represent the 12 patriarchs who ruled the tribes of Israel that Jesus said he had come to restore. Choosing women in this role would not have carried the same significance. This view seems to hold more weight.

However, we could go further and say that although 12 male disciples were named, it is also true that women were among and alongside them. In Luke 8.1 we are told that, 'The twelve were with him, as well as some women …'. These women were an integral part of Jesus' ministry, supporting his work, providing hospitality, probably bankrolling the whole thing. They were not passive observers. Mary, Martha's sister, is commended for sitting at Jesus' feet, the posture of a learning disciple. Mary Magdalene, the first witness of and to the resurrection, was the 'apostle to the apostles' who told her fellow disciples the good news.

And just because Jesus' disciples were all men, it doesn't mean that all the leaders in the Church should be male. The disciples were all first-century Jews, but we don't insist on that criteria for leadership in the Church today. There is clearly in the New Testament a wider vision for ministry and discipleship than just the twelve, a pattern that we do well to reflect in the Church today.

6 If the Bible so positively commends the role of women in the Church, why did the early Church adopt a seemingly male-dominated pattern of leadership after the New Testament period?

There is more evidence than is commonly supposed for women sharing in leadership roles all through Christian history. We can point not only to deacons in the early Church but to the role women have played in the monastic movement (with examples like St Hilda in Britain); the role women have played in the world mission movement, where they were often the pioneers and church planters; and the role women have played down the centuries as evangelists and pastors. The fact that many women were martyred in the sporadic persecution of the Roman Empire is also evidence that they were seen as having positions of responsibility in the Christian community. In every analysis of the reasons why Christianity spread so rapidly across the ancient world, the positive role ascribed within the Christian faith to women – compared to the other faiths of the day – is a significant factor.

It remains true, however, that the Church emerged from the New Testament period with a church leadership that was very largely male, and this has remained the case for many centuries. This is despite the very positive understanding of the role of women alongside men in Scripture that the studies in this book have drawn out. There is no doubt that this was partly because of the role women played in the society of the day. The Church was a small fledgling community. In order to develop and grow in the second and third centuries and throughout the ancient world, it needed to focus its leadership in men, whose voice could and would be heard beyond its own community. In our own day, this argument is reversed: in a world that takes the leadership of women very seriously indeed, not to open all orders of ministry to women and men equally is a hindrance to the gospel.

However, we can also say with hindsight that the Church in the early centuries, like the Church in every generation, did not get everything right. As we saw in Chapter 2, for many centuries Christians did not challenge slavery despite – what seems to us – the clear biblical warrant for all people being created equal and free. In the same way, many believe, Christians accepted a subordinate role for women in ministry for too long and despite – not because of – the Bible's own teaching.

7 Does equality mean that men and women are exactly the same?

No. Women and men were created *as women and men* – male and female. Therefore an element of difference is inherent in our very beings. That is what makes the partnership between male and female in society, the Church and the family so exciting, fruitful and creative. We are not exactly the same. Together we reflect the image of God, and what we bring to each other is our gendered selves.

However, it is notoriously difficult to pin down what the differences actually are. We might be inclined to say that women are more nurturing, more focused on relationship, more approachable, and that men are more prone to risk-taking, more combative and better at map-reading. Indeed, some studies have shown that if one looks at numbers in a given population, these things may be generally, statistically true. But just as men are generally taller than women, some women are taller than some men, and we all know people who do not fit the stereotypes.

It is possible to either under- or overplay the differences between men and women. Denying any sense of difference between maleness or femaleness means we may miss out on the possibilities presented by each. Women and men are not identical nor interchangeable; we need both. But the popular myth that women and men are so different as to have come from different planets (Mars or Venus), and are unable to work together or communicate with each other without considerable help, is taking things too far. We need to warn against the assumptions of biological essentialism – the view that says that everything about the way we behave is biologically determined – and must avoid pinning any of these differences on to particular 'roles' in the Church.

8 Do women exercise leadership differently from men?

Some would say that just as there are general differences between men and women, there are also differences in the way we lead. Women are said to be more collaborative, more empathetic, more caring. There is evidence to suggest that these assumptions have some basis in reality, but again we have to ask whether such differences are innate or formed over time by the expectations placed on us and our own accommodation to perceived norms. Men and women are both prone, because of our sinful state, to exercise authority differently based on customary, but not necessarily healthy, gender roles – men can be dominating and hierarchical, women can be diffident and manipulative.

There is indeed work to be done in recognizing and valuing the gifts both men and women bring to church leadership. Women need to learn to be comfortable with power as well as service, and men need to rediscover characteristics that have been denied them because of their association with the 'feminine', such as vulnerability and empathy. There is a need for both to reclaim those attributes traditionally ascribed to the other in order to liberate both. We will want to challenge the perception that either women or men are more suited to any one particular ministry or way of doing leadership as simply another form of oppression and restriction, recognizing that aspects of a person's make-up other than gender, such as age, life experience and personality, can influence leadership style too.

It is precisely because women are *not* men – and therefore 'different' in some way – that we need both women and men together in ministry in whatever sphere, modelling good practice and living out our call to image God together. We need to be wary of inflexibly attaching any particular quality to women or men uniquely, and to be willing to remove gifts or callings from the terms 'masculine' or 'feminine'. However, it may that many of the so-called feminine traits are exactly what are needed in church leadership today – interpersonal skills, communication, concern for relationship and collaboration.

9 What about the 'feminization' of the Church? If we have more women leaders, won't it put men off the Church?

There is an often loudly stated view that men are leaving the Church because it is too 'feminine' and likely to appeal more to women than men. It is true that there are typically more women than men in church on any given Sunday, but that is nothing new. It's been like that for the past few centuries, especially since the Second World War. Perhaps it has become more stark recently because although women have always been in the majority as *attenders*, in the past the *leaders* were mostly male. Now, however, since the ordination of women, it is a possibility that the leader will be female too, although we need to remember that male leaders still significantly outnumber women in most areas of leadership in the Church.

So it is important to consider what might be meant by 'feminization' when the term is used like this. Some people refer to worship becoming 'touchy-feely' in style, buildings domesticated in appearance and the Church losing its cutting edge, its drive and therefore its appeal to men. But what a church – or society for that matter – considers to be feminine is difficult to pin down and likely to vary from culture to culture. There are many young women who find the 'Jam and Jerusalem' aspects of church off-putting too, and would like to be engaged and challenged with risk and adventure. Young women are leaving the Church too. It is not just a male issue.

That being said, the issue of men in Church is a keen one, and one that needs urgently to be addressed. But limiting women in their roles in the Church is not the way to do it. We do need to find ways as a Church of reaching and addressing the concerns of men, but making the Church more 'masculine' might not be the answer. Neither will making the Church more 'feminine' attract more women.

10 How can women and men work best together in ministry?

The Bible study in Chapter 4 on 1 Timothy 2 pointed out that one of Timothy's concerns was to help the Ephesian church, male and female, to live 'peaceable' lives (2.2) together and within their surrounding society. This would seem to be a good instruction for us as the Church today. Of course, we are fallen and weak human beings and it will be a constant challenge to develop and maintain good working relationships between male and female in ministry, just as forming healthy relationships in all areas of life, society, marriage, family, takes some working at. We will need constantly to check that we are encouraging collaboration not domination, equality not hierarchy and mutual respect not competition. Drawing on God's first command to male and female together to have dominion over the creatures of the earth, this is about partnership, encouragement and support.

Our primary model for church ministry in Scripture is not a hierarchical nuclear family but a body, the parts of which are interdependent and function together. So we need to find ways for men and women to work well together in teams, bringing their contributions as male and female, alike in God's image, to the task of mission and ministry. The Bible is full of good examples of women and men working together to achieve the purposes of God – Deborah and Barack, Esther and Mordecai, Anna and Samuel, Mary, Martha and Lazarus, Priscilla and Aquila.

It is easy to get hung up on gender as the primary difference in working relationships, overlooking the fact that we may be more alike than different as male and female. Difference is just as likely to be about personality, leadership style, team role as it is about gender. So perhaps the first step is to focus on individual people not preconceptions, and to listen carefully to each other.

We will need to be aware of power dynamics if men and women are to work well together. Some have been concerned that women in higher positions of leadership in the Church may be tempted to abuse their power in the same way some men have previously. But with careful and respectful trust in each other, the Church would be blessed by having both men and women leading together in all areas of its life.

11 Why is this such a big issue for the Church at the moment? Aren't there more important matters for us to deal with?

Yes, possibly, but the way we understand women in leadership is linked to all sorts of other ideas about what God is like, what the purpose of humanity is, what the Church is for and how God calls us to live well in the world, as this set of Bible studies has shown. Undoubtedly, there are other very important matters at hand for the Church (the recent census figures showing a significant drop in the number of people declaring themselves to be Christian illustrates this), but having women and men together addressing them will enable the mission of God in the world to be better advanced.

In some parts of the world, equality for women takes on a very different tone. It is a crucially important matter of well-being for whole cultures and societies, where women and girls need to be encouraged and liberated in education, healthcare and public life. Having more women in all places and at all levels of leadership, helping to determine direction and policy in society and Church, is essential for the flourishing of everyone.

Further Reading

If you would like to follow up any of the ideas discussed here, you might find the following books useful.

The most user-friendly and accessible resource is:

Ian Paul, *Women and Authority: The Key Biblical Texts*, Grove Books, 2011. Here you will find a brief overview of the interpretation issues that affect the key passages for discussing the role of women in ministry.

Two other relatively accessible books on the subject are:

Elizabeth Goddard and Clare Hendry, *The Gender Agenda*, InterVarsity Press, 2010. This is a conversation between two friends who disagree in some areas and agree in others. It raises various important issues and looks at all of the key texts.

Derek Tidball and Dianne Tidball, *The Message of Women*, InterVarsity Press, 2012. This looks at women throughout the whole of Scripture and is both thoughtful and devotional in content.

You may want to take your thinking further, in which case you will need to look at some of the more academic books on this subject. Of these, some of the best include:

Linda L. Belleville, *Women Leaders and the Church: Three Crucial Questions*, Revell, 2000.

Richard Clark Kroeger and Catherine Clark Kroeger, *I Suffer Not a Woman: Rethinking I Timothy 2.11–15 in Light of Ancient Evidence*, Baker Publishing Group, 1992.

Philip B. Payne, *Man and Woman, One in Christ*, Zondervan, 2009.

Although technical in parts, another helpful book is:

Linda L. Belleville, Craig L. Blomberg, Craig S. Keener and Thomas R. Schreiner, *Two Views on Women in Ministry*, Zondervan, 2010. In this collection, both sides of the debate are explored by different authors so that you can make up your mind on your own position from their passionately argued views.

The key issue for exploring the relevant biblical texts is the issue of how we interpret the Bible. R. T. France's excellent book uses this subject as a test case for exploring biblical interpretation more widely:

R. T. France, *Women in the Church's Ministry: A Test Case for Biblical Interpretation*, Eerdmans, 1997.

Also interesting is a collection of academic essays that explore the whole subject of biblical equality:

Ronald W. Pierce and Rebecca Merrill Groothuis (eds), *Discovering Biblical Equality: Complementarity Without Hierarchy*, Apollos, 2005.

A fascinating book on Junia is:

Eldon Jay Epp, *Junia: The First Woman Apostle*, 1st edn, Augsburg Fortress, 2005.

Epp goes through all the possible arguments about whether it is more likely that Junia(s) was a woman or a man and what the phrase 'prominent among the apostles' is most likely to mean.

If you become very interested in this subject then it will be important to read some of the most significant arguments *against* the position adopted in this book. For this the following is probably the most helpful:

John Piper and Wayne Grudem (eds), *Recovering Biblical Manhood and Womanhood: A Response to Evangelical Feminism*, Crossway, 2006.

Afterword

Christian Aid has a vision: of a world without poverty. Believing that every person is made in the image of God, we work in over 40 countries for profound change, striving to achieve equality, dignity and freedom for all, regardless of faith, gender or nationality.

The unequal and unfair distribution of power is at the heart of poverty. Recognizing that around 70 per cent of the world's extremely poor people – living on less than $1.25 a day – are women and girls, Christian Aid is working hard to address gender inequality. To take just a few examples, in Bangladesh, Christian Aid is working with partner Christian Commission for Development to empower women through small-scale loan initiatives, while in India, Christian Aid supports Strong Women Alone – a partner working with single, divorced or widowed women who are customarily subjected to discrimination, abuse and exclusion. Christian Aid also works in the Democratic Republic of Congo with the Central Africa Baptist Community who target the army to help end a culture of sexual violence.

Christian Aid is extremely grateful that proceeds from this book will help us make a greater impact on the gender inequality that drives poverty for so many people.